Taking The Bitter
With The Sweet

the story of my life by
Dan Pistoresi — "Mr. P"

DANCING MOON PRESS
NEWPORT, OREGON

Taking The Bitter With The Sweet
the story of my life
copyright © 2014 by Dan Pistoresi, "Mr. P"
All rights reserved (including movie rights)

ISBN-Paperback: 978-1-937493 62-2
Library of Congress Control Number: 2014933529

Book editing and design: *Carla Perry, Dancing Moon Press*
Cover design & production: *Jana Westhusing, StudioBlue/West*
Manufactured in the United States of America

Pistoresi, Dan – "Mr. P"
Taking The Bitter With The Sweet.
1. Autobiography; 2. Family History; 3. Italy; 4. Oregon; 5. Alaska; 6. California; 7. Canada; 8. Las Vegas, Nevada; 9. Philosophy; 10. Advice—car sales; 11. Advice—restaurant business; 12. Advice—marriage, relationships & parenting; 13. Advice—politics; 14. Advice—health & fitness; 15. Advice—grocery shopping; 16. Recipes. I. TITLE.

DANCING MOON PRESS
P.O. Box 832, Newport, OR 97365
541-574-7708
www.dancingmoonpress.com
info@dancingmoonpress.com

First Edition

A special thank you to
Carla Perry, owner of
Dancing Moon Press.

I would not have been able
to finish this book
without her help.

Contents

Introduction: A Smorgasbord of Life

I was inspired to write this autobiography so I could explain some of the things I did during my first fifty years of life. Numerous people told me I could not have done all the things that I claim. But it's all true.

I feel that my story will inspire others to never give up, keep a good attitude, learn how to keep a marriage going, how to treat their children, and how to get along with others. Your marriage will carry out through your children and they will follow about seventy-five percent of the good that goes on, or the bad that you instilled in them while they were growing up. I hope my story conveys how you have to respect others before you can expect others to respect you.

I am still alive and want to tell you how beautiful life can be.

This book is a smorgasbord of my life. I would not have been able to write my story if not for the support of my wonderful family—my lovely wife Elaine, and our children Michael, Danise, Larry, and Paul who left this world on November 1, 2009.

On the left is my uncle—my father's brother. Sitting is my uncle's wife, and on her lap is their daughter, Angelina, who passed away in 2013. My father is standing on the right. This photo was taken in Raymond, Washington, 1918.

Dreaming

I am so proud and happy that I live in the United States of America. The opportunities of bettering ourselves are right in front of us. The dream is to be an independent businessperson. Or the dream could be that you become a doctor, or go to outer space, or that you might be a teacher, a great athlete, or anything else. Whatever comes to your mind, and you like it, then make that your dream. Sometimes dreams do come true. But you have to help in that process.

I have always been a dreamer, and always keep a positive attitude. This is in itself a very good therapy. Sometimes, when it is so peaceful and you are alone, just meditate for a while, and your mind will be clear and this will give you a chance to think straight. Use these moments to try to figure out your ambitions. Maybe you have more than one, and if so, just jot them down and start dreaming the dream you would like to pursue. You might not reach your dream, but you will have fun trying, and do not stop dreaming because some of your dreams will come true.

When I was young, I was afraid of losing one of my parents. I would pray and dream that I would not lose either one of them. Luckily, they both lived to an old age.

I had a dream of getting on a cargo or passenger ship and visiting my cousins in South America by working my way across in exchange for the passage. They said that I was too young. This dream did not come true.

One of my dreams was to own a restaurant and I have now

owned four. I had a dream of operating a photo studio, and I did own one. I dreamed of having a lot of ball teams to sponsor, and that dream came true many times. I dreamed of having a car dealership, and I did have several. I have, for many years, been dreaming about having my own frozen Italian products on the market. This dream has not yet come true. I am 91 years old now and will not give up on this one, because I am still dreaming to have this happen.

My most prominent dream came when I was thinking about marriage. When I was young, I thought that if I ever decided to get married, I would want the marriage to last a lifetime. My beautiful wife, Elaine, and I have been married for 70 years, as of September 14, 2014. This is my best dream.

My mother and father's wedding photo taken in Italy.

Coming To America
And Tragedy On The Titanic

When my mother came over to the United States from Italy in 1922, she had my sister, who was under a year old, with her. There she stood in one of the many queues at Ellis Island, one hand clutching a large, soft leather bag, the other holding her baby daughter. The thief pointed to the bag and then to the table before him. She set it down. He rifled through the contents, but finally rested his finger on the wedding ring she was wearing. He waved his hands towards himself, beckoning the release of her property. It had been her mother's wedding ring, and her grandmother's before that. She looked into his cold eyes and slowly shook her head side to side.

"Mi Dio," she uttered to herself, defiantly denying him the privilege of witnessing her distress. He waved his one hand coldly, as if to dismiss her, while pinning all her immigration papers to the tabletop with the other. She did not budge. Her worries, she realized, were only beginning. What would become of her steamer trunk, stowed somewhere deep in the bellow of the ship? She understood the man's intentions, if not his English, entirely.

"Please?" she managed to implore, but he would have nothing to do with her needs or sentiments. She slowly wrestled the heirloom from her ring finger and gently placed it on the table. The immigration officer snatched the golden treasure and placed it in his jacket pocket. He never looked at her again as he stapled, signed, and pushed the papers back to her across the small table.

Only then was she free to move about in the new country.

I've had friends who told me that what happened to my mother had happened to them. They said such behavior seemed to be the normal way immigrants were treated as they entered the country. "This is what happened in the early 1920s."

My son Michael said my parents were cut of a certain cloth—strong material that bound the family together. They were cautiously generous, mindful with purpose, and deliberate in everything they did. Michael said their attitude showed even in the way his grandpa cut the Prosciutto he had already painstakingly cured—sliced into paper-thin slices—which spoke volumes of the little pleasures he found in life. A patient couple they were.

The basement of the home I grew up in was wide open, with a wine press, a wine cellar, and many other utilitarian features. Its solid foundation easily held the manor-style arts and craft dwelling, with its mounded yard full of every type of flower, vegetable and poultry you could possibly imagine. This made me feel so good, because of my son Michael's comments.

One of my mother's sisters married Nello Barsotti. One sister married a Malaca from Fresno, California. The other sister lived in Italy. Many Italian families have had an influence on the development of Madera, California, and Madera County. Their names have become familiar to the people. Some I will mention: Baraldi, Logoluso, Del Bono, Baratta, Del Bianco, Bernardi, Dellavalle, Cimino, Montanari, Boitano, Stefanelli, Crappa, Ferrarese, Lukesi, Cappelluti, Bomprezzi, Farinelli, Biancalana, Paravagna, Ferretti, Noli, Manfredi, Dominici, Brunetti, Sciacqua, Brunolli, Caregaino, Franco, La Mattina, Marcini, Poletti, Oliva, Simi, Sordi, Pistoresi, Toschi, Massetti, Tabour, Tordini, Varbella, Franzoia, Raviscioni, Spennli, Martinelli, Armi, Oberti, Massaco, Maggiorini, Grattone, Longatti, Andfrachi, Barsotti.

In 1900, Dominic Barsotti came over from Italy to America, settling first in Stockton, California. Then in 1902, he was joined by his son Nello, then twelve years old, and with his father went to Firebaught, where they established a small hotel. A few years later, Mrs. Barsotti and her three daughters came over and joined them in 1906. They had two more daughters. They made Madera, California, their permanent home.

The Barsottis established a hotel in Madera where the standard garage on North F. Street now stands. This was known as the Barsotti and Son Hotel. Their youngest son, Albert, now the mayor of Madera, was born in 1916. After a while, the Barsottis decided to sell the hotel and go into the bakery business. They built the building now occupied by Francis Price Bakery.

Some of the Barsottis still live in Madera.

All of this information is from the Madera *News Tribune* newspaper as of 1957. If I missed someone, or misspelled your name, I sincerely apologize to you. History still goes on and I am very proud of all these people I mentioned. I am very proud that I was born in Madera, California, on December 19, 1923.

The one thing I feel sorry about is that I never did get the honor to meet or ever see my grandparents on my mother's or my father's side. I was in Bari, Italy, during the war, and this was as close as I could get to see my grandparents. They lived in northern Italy and they were still fighting there. We are very lucky and happy to be able to see our grandchildren and great grandchildren. We get to see them and we enjoy being around them.

One of my mother's sisters, Argene Genovesi, was married to Sebastino Del Carlo. They were married in Lucca, Italy. They were determined to seek a new life in the United States, so they made their way to Cherbourg and purchased two second-class tickets on the maiden voyage of the Titanic. This was to be their honeymoon.

They had no way of knowing that four days later, one of history's greatest tragedies would end their bliss.

FEATURES

PAGE B1 MADERA TRIBUNE Tuesday, February 2, 2010

PIECES OF THE PAST
By Bill Coate

Taking the Titanic to Madera

MY MOTHERS NAME WAS NOT MENTIONED, CATERINA GENOVESI PISTORES

It took a while for panic to take hold of the passengers of the Titanic. Nobody believed the ship could sink, lest of all Sebastino del Carlo and his bride, Argene. Nothing could happen to them; they were coming to America-to California-to Madera.

Sebastino del Carlo and Argene Genovesi had been engaged on Jan. 20, 1912, and one month later they were married in Lucca, Italy. By April they had determined to seek a new life in a new land, so they made their way to Cherbourg and purchased two second-class tickets on the maiden voyage of the Titanic. This was to be their honeymoon. They had no way of knowing that four days later one of history's greatest tragedies would end their bliss.

Sebastino had decided to come to Madera because his new brother-in-law, Nello Barsotti, had found him a job in a bakery. Nello had married Eugenia Genovesi, Argene's sister, and the prospect of having another sister close by thrilled the local couple (a third sister, Carolina Gen-

MADERA COUNTY HISTORICAL SOCIETY

This photograph of Sebastino del Carlo and Argene Genovesi was taken on Feb. 20, 1912, their wedding day. In less than two months they were on their way to Madera aboard the Titanic. Needless to say they didn't make it, he perished in the disaster, and though she survived, she turned back to live out her life in her native Italy.

ovesi Malanca and her husband, John, lived in Fresno). When news came of the impending arrival of the del Carlos, the Barsottis prepared for a reunion — a reunion that never came.

On April 11, 1912, the Titanic set sail with the del Carlos aboard. Unfortunately, Argene was forced to stay in her cabin due to nausea, which left her unable to enjoy the trip. It would, however, get considerably worse.

Just before midnight on April 14, 1912, Argene heard a loud noise and felt a shudder. She called for Sebastino to find out what had happened. When he reached the deck, he discovered their dilemma and hurried back to the cabin.

Without much conversation, Sebastino lifted his wife in his arms and carried her topside. There, as the crew gently placed the ill woman in one of the lifeboats, he kissed her and told her not to worry; he assured her they would be reunited very soon. As the lifeboat was lowered, Sebastino waved goodbye, and a tearful Argene returned the wave. That was not the last time she would see him, but it was the last time she would

SEE TITANIC, PAGE B2

My mother's sister was on the Titanic.

Titanic

CONTINUED FROM PAGE B1

see him alive.

As everybody knows, in the early hours of April 15, 1912, the Titanic sank, and 1,517 people lost their lives. One of these was Sebastino del Carlo.

The survivors, including Argene, were rescued by the Carpathia and taken to New York, where she was cared for by a Catholic relief organization. Meanwhile, Sebastino's body continued to float in the frigid waters near the site of the sinking. He remained there for a couple of days until the MacKay Bennett, one of the recovery ships, pulled him from the ocean.

They delivered Sebastino to a makeshift morgue in New York and then brought Argene there to identify his remains. He was still clothed in his dark, tweed suit and wrapped in his gray overcoat. Beside him were the personal effects that he had taken with him from the ship: a gold watch and chain; a pair of diamond and gold earrings, a gold chain locket; a silver watch and chain; a knife; a pin; a pocketbook and papers along with $5 in notes and 37 francs.

Now Argene had a decision to make. Should she bury her husband in New York and continue to California alone, or should she take him back to Italy and remain in her homeland. Argene chose the latter.

On May 18, 1912, Argene boarded the Cretic and accompanied Sebastino's body back to Italy where she buried him. In four short months she had gone from an engagement to a wedding to widowhood. In a few more months, however, new life would spring from the horror of the sinking of the Titanic. You see, when she embarked on the doomed vessel with her husband, Argene was expecting, and by that time, in addition to seasickness, the ill effects of her pregnancy confined her to her room on the

WHITE STAR LINE

BOARDING PASS

PERMISSION GRANTED TO COME ABOARD

WHITE STAR LINE'S

R.M.S.

TITANIC

ISMAY, IMRIE & CO.,
34, LEADENHALL STREET, LONDON,
AND
10, WATER STREET, LIVERPOOL

MADERA COUNTY HISTORICAL SOCIETY

This boarding pass allowed Sebastino and Argene to board the Titanic at Cherbourg on April 11, 1912. They set sail for America the next day but never made it. The pass indicates they enjoyed 2nd class accommodations until the ship struck an iceberg.

Titanic. On Nov. 14, 1912, Argente gave birth to a daughter, Salvata del Carlo.

When Sebastino carried his young bride to the lifeboat on April 15, 1912, he knew he held both his wife and his child in his arms. Although she was still in the womb, Salvata was the youngest survivor of the sinking of the Titanic.

The shock waves of the Titanic disaster reverberated around the world, and nowhere were they felt any stronger than in Madera. Eugenia Genovesi Barsotti and her husband, Nello, grieved over Argene's loss, and over the years, all of the Barsotti

children in Madera learned the story of how fate stepped in to keep their aunt and uncle from coming here to live.

Meanwhile, Salvata grew up in Italy, married, and became a mother herself. Then a strange thing happened. Director James Cameron decided to make a movie and called it "Titanic." This turned her nation's spotlight on the lady who would have called Madera her home if only her parents had taken a different boat to America.

• • •

THE STORY OF HOW SALVATA BECAME THE OBJECT OF NATIONAL INTEREST IN ITALY AND HOW IT AFFECTED HER RELATIVES IN MADERA WILL BE TOLD IN NEXT WEEK'S PIECES OF THE PAST.

Sebastino had decided to come to Madera, California, to work for his brother-in-law, Nello Barsotti, in his bakery. Nello was married to my mother's sister, Eugenia Genovesi. It would have been nice to have all the sisters close by. One of the sisters, Carolina Genovesi, was married to John Malanca. They lived in Fresno. A reunion that never came.

On April 11, 1912, the Titanic set sail with the Del Carlos aboard. Unfortunately, Argene was forced to stay in her cabin due to nausea, which left her unable to enjoy the trip. It would, however, get considerably worse. Just before midnight on April 14, 1912, my aunt heard a loud noise and felt a shudder. She called for Sebastino to find out what was happening. When he reached the deck, he discovered their dilemma and hurried back to the cabin. Without much conversation, Sebastino lifted his wife in his arms and carried her topside. There, as the crew gently placed my aunt in one of the lifeboats, he kissed her and told her not to worry. He assured her that they would be reunited very soon. As the lifeboat was lowered, Sebastino waved goodbye and Argene returned the wave, in tears. That was not the last time she would see him, but it was the last time she would see him alive.

As everybody knows, in the early hours of April 15, 1912, the Titanic sank and 1,517 people lost their lives. One of these was Sebastino Del Carlo. One of the survivors was my Aunt Argene. The people on her lifeboat were rescued by the Carpathia and taken to New York where she was cared for by a Catholic relief organization.

Meanwhile, Sebastino's body continued to float in the frigid waters near the site of the sinking. He remained there for a couple of days until the MacKay Bennett, one of the recovery ships, pulled him from the ocean. They delivered his body to a makeshift morgue in New York and brought Argene to identify his remains. He was still clothed in his dark tweed suit and wrapped in his gray overcoat. All his personal effects were beside him.

My aunt had to make a decision—to bury her husband in New York and continue to California alone, or take him back to Italy and remain in her homeland. She chose to go back to Italy.

On May 18, 1912, my aunt boarded the Cretic, and took her husband's body back to Italy where she buried him. However, a new life would spring from the horror of the sinking of the Titanic. My aunt was expecting, and on November 14, 1912, she gave birth to a daughter, Salvata. When Sebastino carried his young bride to the lifeboat, he was also carrying his daughter in his wife's womb. Salvata was the youngest survivor on the Titanic. My mother and her sisters were very sad that their sister was not going to join them; they had hoped they could all be together.

Meanwhile, Salvata grew up in Italy, married, and became a mother herself. Then a strange thing happened. Somebody decided to make a movie and called it *Titanic*. This turned the nation's spotlight on my aunt who would have called Madera, California, her home 100 years ago.

I want to give credit where credit is due: to Bill Coate of the Madera *Tribune*. I took most of this information from his well-written article about the *Titanic*.

My Aunt Argene, in Italy, kept in close contact with my Aunt Eugenia Barsotti in Madera, and kept in contact with my cousin Gloria Massetti about twice a year. Salvata joined in this communication with her Madera relatives. My parents lived in Portland, Oregon, and did miss out on a lot of this.

Then in 1965, my Uncle Nello and Aunt Eugenia took their daughter Gloria and her husband Angelo Massetti to Italy to see Argene and Salvata, the aunt and cousin they had been communicating with all these years. The reunion was not about the

Titanic. Most of the conversation was centered on the family, both in Italy and in America. My aunt wished that she would have continued her trip to Madera, California, instead of going back to Italy. My aunt died in 1970. My cousin Gloria and Angelo kept in close touch with Salvata for another 25 years or so, and then a strange thing happened.

Salvata was 85 years old when the movie *Titanic,* starring Leonardo DiCaprio, was released in 1997. Until that time, Salvata had lived a quiet life in her native Italy. But when the film came out, she became the object of the media spotlight since her mother was onboard and pregnant at the time of the disaster. Technically, Salvata had been aboard the Titanic. Hence, the public interest in her when the blockbuster movie was released. The family did not expect the firestorm that the movie created for them, but it descended on them nevertheless. The granddaughter informed my cousin Gloria about how the Italian press went after her grandmother's story. A newspaper called them to see if they could get an interview, and they accepted. And after the article appeared in the papers, they had no peace. Many news reporters came from all over, plus from the TV stations that gave them a big party. A famous baker, who works only for actors and singers, baked a very large cake with the Titanic theme.

Salvata lived a good long life in Italy. She died in 2008, and one of the most exciting things she took with her to the grave was the vivid memories of the Titanic that had been imbedded in her mind by her mother who, in the end, wished she had continued her journey to Madera, California.

Growing Up In Portland, Oregon

I was born on December 19, 1923, in Madera, California. My father, mother, and sister were born in northern Italy. My father's brother was in the United States working for the railroad, and he decided to go back to Italy to be with his father and mother.

My mother had two sisters living in Fresno and Madera, California, and a sister living in Italy.

My father drove a bakery delivery truck for his brother-in-law, delivering to out-of-town stores. My uncle told me when I was growing up that the bakery business was the most profitable business to get involved in.

When I was two years old, my parents decided to move to Portland, Oregon. My sister Sara was born with one leg four inches shorter than the other leg and a dislocated hip. She was a patient at the Shriners Hospital where Dr. Dillehunt was the head of the hospital, and he operated on my sister five times.

By the time that Dr. Dillehunt had completed all the operations, her leg was only a quarter of an inch shorter than the other one. My father and mother would take a box of oranges to the hospital and give them out. The staff made them feel like they had given them a million dollars.

Because of all the time that my sister spent in the hospital as a child, she was twenty years old when she graduated from high school. She decided to go into the nursing field. She was in the first graduating class of licensed practical nurses in the state of Oregon.

She was gifted with healing hands and was considered the top in her field. She always had a positive attitude and never in her lifetime was she ever with a negative thought or ever felt sorry for herself. She was a member of the Chin Up Club.

My father, Guy Pistoresi, my mother, Catherine Pistoresi, and my sister Sara. My father always wore a tie on Sunday.

We were so lucky to have such great parents. We did not have much money in the house. We had lots of love and great food. My mother and father were great cooks. My father enlisted in the Army during World War I and he was so proud to become an American citizen.

My father used to make his own wine, like most Europeans did, and he let me help him put the grapes in the vat to be pressed. My father would give us a glass of water with a tablespoon of wine when we ate dinner, and as we got older, he would give me half and half, then later, a full glass of wine. He explained to me that he wanted to teach me how to drink and enjoy it and to know when you had enough to drink. He told me never drink too much so that I would not make a fool of myself. My father was never drunk and I have never been drunk. In my thinking, if you drink, do it when you are feeling happy, not when you are sad. When I drink, it is because I enjoy a few cocktails.

My parents taught me manners and I have never forgotten. I taught the same to my family. Most important: be kind with others.

My father had a great operatic voice and knew a lot about music. His friend next door was a teacher of music and told me that my father knew more about music and operas than he did. When he was a boy, my father asked to study music at a music school, but his parents would not let him go. I am glad that they made that decision or I would have missed having such a great father.

My father worked for the gas company making briquettes, a very dirty job, and he had to take a shower when he got off work. Then he worked for Eastern and Western Lumber Company, pulling lumber off the green chain, which was a very hard job. He worked there for over twenty years, and the company decided to close the mill. He ended up without a job. He could have gone to work at the shipyards and made a lot more money during the war, but he had wanted to be faithful to the company that he worked for and ended up without a job. They were not faithful to him.

He went to the city of Portland and got a job sweeping the streets. And after having that job for a short time, they told him that he had to take a civil service exam. He did not finish school in Italy, so he was not able to pass the test so he lost his job. They had been really lucky to have him.

I really get a kick out of the way people talk about profiling. They always are profiling people. They will never stop. By your last name alone, and your religion, you are profiled. This has caused many people to take on an English name such as Jones, Smith, York, George, Harvey, and you name it. I am so happy that my father and mother did not change their name from Pistoresi. I really would have lost faith in them. Nowadays, things are a lot better. Your last name makes less difference when applying for a position than it did in the past. And thank God for this. We are slowly learning how to appreciate each other. But not enough.

My father was making $90 to $110 per month, and my mother did not have to go to work. My father loved to drive his 1926 Ford Model T. My parents purchased a house for $1,100 with $50 down and made $10 per month payments. My parents were very protective of their children. They did not want us to go into the house of someone we did not know. I hope more people will do the same for their children. I think people back then were more relaxed and took things a lot less seriously than we now do nowadays. Families seemed to enjoy life more because everyone got involved. It was not a dog-eat-dog situation like we have now.

Education

If I had the authority to hire the teachers of our children, I would demand a background check on every one of them to make sure that what they teach does not include their hang-ups. We cry wolf when it is too late.

A teacher obviously has a lot to do with helping our children achieve a good education. Schools should not try to brainwash students because some of the teachers hired to fill positions are not smart enough to hold a teacher's certificate. A little knowledge can be very dangerous. Because they passed the tests and received their certification, does not mean they are qualified to teach. Of course, we do have some great teachers and I respect those and think very highly of them. However, some of the low-life teachers do more harm to students who depend on them for their education. Those teachers cause problems. Some teachers go into their profession for reasons other than to teach.

Parents should always quiz their children on how they are getting along with their teacher. If something is negative, it's best to nip it in the bud right away and find out what the problem is. Maybe it is just the student that created the problem, not the teacher.

My first Holy Communion.

During the summer, on Sundays, my parents would take us on a picnic or for a drive out of town. This was always a family outing. My parents would never think of having a babysitter watch us or letting someone else take care of my sister and I. They would not trust anyone to watch over us kids.

I was very bashful and afraid of the dark, and when I went to bed, I would sleep with the covers over my head because I was very scared. When I printed the alphabet, the letters were printed backwards. It took a lot of effort and work to print them the correct way. My mother could not speak very good English, so I always spoke Italian at home. My mother was a homebody and her devotion was to her family.

I believe that most foreign-speaking people during those days made sure their children would write with their right hand even though they were left-handed, and I think my parents might have done it with me because I kicked the football and the soccer ball with my left foot. I always did want to be left-handed. Playing basketball, I could shoot with my left and right hand. When I played tennis, I would serve with my right hand, but slice it to the left side. I might have had dyslexia.

My parents told me to never start a fight or lose my temper. It is easier to talk your problem out and remain friends. Brains over brawn, and you can still keep your macho status if that means so much to you. Because, in the real world, it means zilch. My mother told me to laugh when someone teased me, and in no time, the taunting had stopped because they could not get to me. Mother was right, that reaction does work.

I was teased and called a lot of names that were not very nice, and some of them I would not want to mention. I was called lop ear because one of my ears stuck out more than my other ear. I was called wop, mafia, dago, and catlicker because of being Catholic.

The letters W-O-P were put on people at Ellis Island that meant without passport. The teasing and name-calling did not really bother me that much, but what really did bother me was when they would call my sister cripple crap, plus a lot of nasty words. These bullies were very rude and crude. There always had to be more than one of them before they would have the courage to say anything because they were cowards. The sad part about it is that the cowards always had some weak-minded followers.

I did become a little self-conscious because of the bullying. My mother told me to consider the source, and that did help me. I went to St. Philip Neri Catholic Grade School, and my first four years there I did well with my grades. When I was in the sixth grade, I did not do very good. I had to stay after school many times.

When it came time to get our report cards, which occurred every six weeks, they handed them out according to grades. This was terrible on me because I was one of the last to receive my report card. This was very cruel. It should be private between teacher and pupil. I think it is nice to praise the top boy and girl in the class and leave it at that. I always felt defeated in this class. Your grades have nothing to do with anybody else's grades. This can give you a complex. I was no scholar. I really did not like to do my homework and I did very little of it. Which did not help my grades in school.

I was very good at my multiplication. But I had to write on the blackboard for one hour because I could not recite a poem. I felt bad enough because I had a hard time with poems, and at that time poetry seemed a little sissy to me. I learned the preamble, and I am still able to recite it.

I now really appreciate poetry and enjoy listening to others read and reading it myself. I wish I had felt the same way when I was younger. Maybe if I'd an understanding teacher, I might not have had problems back then with poetry.

One day, someone shot a spit wad at the nun and she accused me of doing it. I jumped out of my seat, raised my right hand, and said, "Honest, Sister. I did not do it." I was so shattered that she would not believe me! I explained to my parents what happened to me and they felt as bad as I did. I mentioned to my parents that I would not feel good by staying and knowing that my nun did not believe in me. My parents took me out of St. Philip Neri Catholic School, and from there I started at a public school, Brooklyn School.

I knew who shot the spit wad at the nun, and if she would have taken a little time, she could have found out who did it. I was very polite to her. I always wondered, even to this day, why she treated me the way she did. After I left the school, I really felt sorry for the nun. She might have had a sad family life. I was the most polite student at school, and polite away from school.

In growing up, I never ever heard my mother or father run down anybody because of their race, color, or their religion. I did not know the word prejudice. We lived very close to the railroad tracks and a lot of fellows riding the rails would knock on our door for a handout. My mother would make up some sandwiches and fruit to give them. We could not give them any money because we did not have much ourselves. We never did turn anybody down. But we would never let any of them come into the house. We would have them wait outside while my mother made their lunch. I asked one of the hoboes how did he know where to stop for a handout. He said our house was marked so others would know who might feed them.

My mother baked homemade bread, and after she took it out of the oven and while it was still hot, she would get some dishes and pour olive oil, wine vinegar, salt, and pepper in them. We would dip the warm bread into the mix. It was so good! Most of the time she would boil the meat or chicken and make soup, then slice the meat to eat. Her soups always had vegetables. Her stews were out of this world. Some of my friends would tell me that they liked my mother's cooking and her baked bread.

We had some Italian-speaking women who wanted to buy some of her bread. Some of my friends asked me if they could eat at our house because they liked my mother's cooking. Hearing this from my friends really made me feel very proud of my mother. I was always very proud of my mother and this gave it an extra kicker. She was such a kind person and would always help anyone as much as she could. We had chickens, rabbits, sheep, and a goat. Rabbit meat is very good to eat.

Sometimes we would have company over for dinner and my mother would prepare roast beef, roast chicken, pasta, cutlets, potatoes cooked in with the roast, salad, dessert, and then, of course, my dad's homemade wine. My mother did this all on a small woodstove. To this day, I do not know how she did it. When you are young, you take this all for granted.

She sure knew how to shop for groceries. We would never buy hamburger. We would grind our own meat. The butcher always made sure the meat was very fresh because he knew that my mother was very fussy, even if it was only ten or thirty cents worth of meat she was buying. When you purchased meat, they would throw in soup bones at no charge. Most people would say they wanted the bones for their dog. But this would be after they made their soup. There was always a little meat on the bones. When I would go to the meat market and buy meat she did not like, she would have me take it back to get a better cut. I was sixteen years old before I ate my first hamburger.

My father would plant his garden and it would always look like a showplace by the time he was through. Nothing is better than picking a tomato off the vine and having a saltshaker with you. This way, you know that it is fresh and you would get that smell and taste of a real tomato.

We only had an icebox to keep meat, fish, and milk cold. The ice was delivered once or twice a week, depending on how hot it was. The ice would come in blocks of 25 or 50 pounds. When we needed ice, we would have a sign on our door showing how much ice we wanted to buy. We did not have electricity. We had gaslight in the house we lived in at that time.

Most of the fruit was sold by the dozen. Potatoes and apples were sold by the bushel or by the sack. Most homes had a fruit tree or two, and a small garden. It is getting more crucial now that you need to plant fruit trees and have a garden to grow your own clean and healthy vegetables. My mother and father would have their own seeds from the year or two before and get a box or container with dirt and compost, plant the seeds, and put a piece of glass over it, which makes it a simplified hot house. I fear inflation because the economy is just about as bad as during a war. The bubble has burst and they keep blowing it back up to burst again.

When watermelons were in season, we would walk a couple of miles to the produce outlet to see if they had any cracked melons. And if they did, they would give them to us. One out of every two or three trips we would score. This was well worth the walk for us. They would give us apples if there were little bruises on them. This was not always a total loss, going to the produce outlet.

My father took me to the slaughterhouse with him and he'd get all the meats he needed to make Italian sausage, headcheese, and for curing his own Prosciutto. Every day, he would go down to the basement to cure it with salt and pepper, and I think he would talk to the Prosciutto. When it was all cured and ready to eat, my father would slice it paper thin and we would eat it with figs and melons when the melons were in season. This was as good as you could eat.

31

During the smelt run on the Sandy River, you could catch a bucket of smelt in a very short time. My father would prepare the smelt with a light batter, fry them in olive oil, and then marinate them. They were so delicious prepared this way. The smelt is a white fish and is very tasty.

The fruits and vegetables are priced too high now, and this alone should encourage you to grow your own. If you have the space, you should plant your own garden and have a couple of fruit trees. This way, you will not have to worry where the produce comes from or who packed it. We must all be concerned about the fertilizers used on our food. When you purchase any vegetables or fruit, make sure you double wash them before you think of cooking or eating them. This can be very serious to your health if you do not take some of these tips. Eating fresh vegetables and fruit while I was growing up really helped me stay in good health.

I always ran with a softball or tennis ball in my hands, throwing it up in the air and catching it. I never walked slow, except when going to church. We played roller skate hockey and softball on the street. I did not have a bike, but someone gave me a bike frame but even still, I could not afford to get the rest of the parts to fix it up.

One of my friends had a chance to work for Western Union delivering telegrams and he did not have a bike of his own. He told me that if I would let him use my frame, he would furnish the parts to fix it up. I was supposed to get it back in three months, but my friend still did not have enough money to buy his own bike, so I let him use it for two more months. The two months seemed like a year. I did end up having my own bike to ride.

When I was playing sports, I always wanted to play with someone better than I was. This way I would have the opportunity to learn and get better at the sport. We played basketball on the street corner with a five-gallon paint can hollowed out, using a tennis ball. Later, we upgraded to a ball that was five inches in diameter and, finally, we all chipped in and purchased a utility basketball that was designed for street use. This was a great achievement for us.

Before we started school the next semester, the decision was made to turn it into a girl's high school. The Parent Teachers Association (PTA) fought tooth and nail to stop the closure. We had a court hearing, and Mrs. Salerno, the mother of one of the students, fought very hard to keep our school open. Some of us kids went on strike, and we went to the courthouse to listen to what was going on about trying to keep our school open. We would walk downtown to the courthouse and each buy five cents worth of peanut brittle to eat in the courtroom. That was until Honorable Judge Olson told us not to eat in the courtroom anymore. He told us we made too much noise eating candy. He was a very well respected judge.

Some of my friends went back to school within two weeks. I stayed out for a month. I started at Llewelyn Grade School, which was about three miles away from home. They gave streetcar and trolley bus tickets for kids who lived at least ten blocks from where they could catch a ride. They allowed us a roundtrip fare that cost four and a half cents each way.

The Assistant Superintendent of schools in Portland, Oregon, Mr. Dougdale, was visiting our school and I was called into the principal's office. They wanted to take away my transportation fare to be able to attend school. They said I did not live ten or more blocks from where I could board my ride. I told them that my parents would not let me cross the busy street in front of our house unless I would cross at a safety lane. Going either direction, I would be about fourteen blocks from where I could cross. If I lived across the street from our house, I would have been only nine blocks from boarding a bus, and I would not have been allowed to receive transportation fare. Mr. Dougdale told the principal before we started that I would have a good story for why they should allow me to keep getting my bus tickets. I did keep getting my bus tickets.

Most of my friends went to Sacred Heart Catholic School and some to other public schools. My friends wanted me to go to Sacred Heart. The public schools had a seven A and seven B class. I was in the seven B, and told my friends that I did not want to go back to the seventh grade. Knowing that the Catholic schools are much harder than the public schools, I wanted to see if I could start in the eighth grade class. My friends wanted me to talk to the nun. I did get to meet Sister Mary Margaret and explained my situation and why I was concerned. She told me that if I kept a positive attitude and studied, I should have no problem fitting in. She advised me to set goals, and mentioned that if I did not make my goal, I should not be disappointed, but just try a little harder.

I did enroll and got my best grades ever. The school had a two-year high school course. They had fewer than ten students, and two of the boys were scholars—Paul Monfils and John Giannini. From the two-year course, they went to Washington High School, which had 2,000 students. John Giannini became student body president.

While I was still in the eighth grade, we had a very good basketball team and we always practiced in the gym. One day that we wanted to practice, the girls had the gym and we started to give them a bad time. After lunch break, we went back to class, and Sister Margaret called four of us out of the classroom and really gave us a tongue-lashing. Al Milligan was laughing, and Sister hit him on the chin, which caused Joe Lair to start laughing, and then I started to laugh because it was funny the way she hit Al. She grabbed Joe's arm, twisted it, and told me I was next. Every time I think of this, I burst out laughing. We were in the wrong and we should have known better. We did know better.

Sister Margaret was very strict and she really earned respect from us all. Teachers could learn more about teaching from her than they could learn from college. I would giver her a solid ten for teaching and a solid ten for being an outstanding nun.

When we wanted to practice basketball in the gym after school, I was always elected to ask Father Gregory for permission to use it. Every time I would ask him, he would say no. Then I would mention that the public school was very close by and that we wanted to beat them in basketball and how bad it would look if they beat us.

When Father would agree to let us practice in the gym, he would want us to have on only one string of lights and not use the showers. Later, he would come in the hall and see two strings of lights on, and steam coming from the shower room. I think he really got a kick out of this because he went through this every time we wanted to use the hall. He never did get angry with us. He was a terrific pastor.

The University of Oregon and Oregon State University played pre-season games against an independent team in our basketball hall. The Harlem Globetrotters also played here.

The girls had a great basketball team. They won over sixty straight games and after that, I do not think they ever lost a game. During that time, girls played half court. Some of them became very good basketball players. This was in 1937 and 1938.

Father Gregory gave us permission to build a tennis court and we all helped build it. Father Paul, who was under Father Gregory, was a very good tennis player, and taught us a lot about playing tennis and we all got to be fairly good at it. We would buy used tennis balls, and some of the tennis clubs would give us used balls.

Playing tennis.

The hall where we played basketball had been a graphic arts studio. Clark Gable, who was not yet a famous actor, and many artists worked out of there. Clark Gable worked at a lumberyard with my friend's father in Portland.

Next door to the Aladdin Theater was a restaurant, and on one side they had a poolroom with two pool tables, and I was the house man. If someone beat me, he would not have to pay for the game, but if I beat him, he would have to pay double. I would win about eight out of ten times. No liquor was sold any place nearby. Some ladies called the police on us for being in a pool hall. Because of the complaint, the restaurant owner made us quit playing pool. He did not want it this way, but he was put on the spot. I never did get any pay for this, but I got to play a lot of pool.

We would go on vacant property and look for empty whiskey bottles. We would get five cents each for them.

During the summer, I would develop and print pictures for customers. With the little profit I made, I would buy 25 or 50 cents worth of pennies and go through them to try and find a rare one. I have found a 1909 SVDB, 1914 D, 1931 S, and 1926. When I was lucky enough to find these, I would sell them to a coin dealer. On a 1909 SVDB, I would get 75 cents to a dollar-fifty, depending on condition. Most of the time I would get ten to twenty-five cents for other coins. One dollar would buy twenty-four Hershey or Baby Ruth candy bars. I even sold the *Seattle P-I* (Post-Intelligencer) Sunday newspaper in Portland, Oregon. People would ask me why they should buy an out-of-state paper, and I would tell them they could find out what was happening in the state of Washington. I sold *Liberty* magazine and other magazines door-to-door.

Parents should try to encourage their children to have a hobby of some kind while they are growing up. This way, it makes it easy for them to get involved. A few hobbies that are a lot of fun and very popular are coins, stamps, books, magazines, sport cards, comic books, model cars, airplanes, and many other collectables. When you collect stamps, this will give you the opportunity to learn about other countries, learn how to be patient, and absorb a lot of knowledge. You will learn something about business, and it teaches you how to barter and helps you keep a clear head so you will be able to think for yourself.

Hobbies will help you to be self-disciplined and provides an excellent way for keeping kids off drugs and staying out of trouble. Many people own their business because of a hobby they got involved with growing up and are still having a lot of fun doing it, while making money. Cooking is one of the best hobbies. Some chefs make six figures plus per year.

During the Depression in the 1930s, my father-in-law raised three boys and one daughter. Because of his stamp hobby, he was able to put food on the table and make his house payments. He was very credible. Credibility is the most honorable asset you have to have to be an honest businessperson and a good respected citizen.

A block away from my home was a vacant field. A private dairy had a few cows grazing on this land. My friends and I would play tackle football when the cows were not grazing and sometimes we would end up in cow pies. This did not make our mothers very happy. We purchased our milk from this very small dairy.

The King Brothers Boiler Works was across the street from our house and the train tracks were next to the dairy. There was a small stockyard nearby so when the cattle cars arrived they would unload the cattle so the animals could have water, hay, and some rest. When the cattle cars were transporting horses, the cowboys would let us get on the horses and walk them around.

When we walked to the downtown area of Portland, we got there by walking the railroad tracks, and just across the bridge was a soda shop where you could get a milkshake and see a cowboy movie for fifteen cents, which we did when we could afford it. If a train was coming, we would run and grab onto the ladder to hitch a ride. This was really a very dumb and dangerous thing to do.

Every month, the Aladdin Theater would publish their program schedule to show what would be playing that month. My friends and I would receive tickets for three movies in exchange for delivering their programs door-to-door to every house in our district. The leader would get four free tickets. Not much later, I was getting four tickets.

All public parks in the Portland area had softball teams based on each kid's height. Playing at these different parks, we had a chance to meet some real nice guys. Not once did any fights break out. We all loved sports so much that we learned how to win well and take a loss with dignity. We all like to win, but there's always a loser and you just have to try a little harder the next time. Always try to control your own emotions.

When we did not play at the park, some of the business owners would furnish sweatshirts, softballs, gloves, and a stencil for their names to appear on the sweatshirts. All of this was furnished by two or three sponsors. This really took a lot of work, trying to get the sponsors lined up. I am talking about strong companies that were very tight with their support. For the little they put out, they tried to make us think they were giving us a million dollars. I said to myself that someday I hoped I would be in a position to sponsor a lot of ball teams.

I think deep down I wanted to be a junior Abe Saperstein, a person I never had the pleasure of meeting. Saperstein owned the famous Harlem Globetrotters basketball team. When I was in Boy Scout Troop #82, my folks had enough money to buy only the shirt; we couldn't afford the pants. Later, someone gave me the pants. I think we were one of the poorest Boy Scout troops in Portland.

There was going to be a Scout Jamboree at Washington Park and I mentioned this to the Scoutmaster. I told him that no one really knew who we are, and I came up with the idea to have a question mark printed on our neckerchief, and he went along with it. We did get a lot of attention and curiosity. Sometimes you have to come up with new ideas.

I grew up in the Brooklyn district of southeast Portland and we would hang out around Powell Boulevard and Milwaukie Avenue. We would go to the drugstore, and for ten cents, we could buy a large bottle of Par-T-Pak soda with two glasses filled with ice and sit at the counter to drink it. This was a great treat for us. The owners of the drugstore were very nice to all of us. The people who owned the bakery next door were also very nice. There were a lot of Nazi bunds in Oregon and we always thought that the drugstore and the bakery owners were involved with the bund movement. A very good friend of mine told me his father used to go to the meetings held in the drugstore's back room. There were a lot of Irish, German, and Italians living in our area. We had Nazi and Fascist sympathizers all around us. This was in 1937 to 1939 that all this took place.

I had two friends who wanted to finish their schooling in Germany and we were invited to a going-away party for them. I did not give it a thought until a couple of years later when they went to Germany to fight for Hitler (this is my own opinion). I was not rude, but when I would hear people brag about their mother country, I would tell them that they should go back there.

I was so happy that my father joined the American Army and wanted to be an American citizen. When I hear our own people run down our beautiful country, I think about setting up a fund to buy them a one-way ticket to wherever they want to go. We must teach our children to respect our country, or whatever country they live in. Many people left their home country to come to live in the greatest country in the world because they knew it was going to be a better place to live and raise a family. Very few ever wanted to go back to where they came from, and if they did decide to go back, in most cases it was because they were homesick or because their parents were aging and wanted to live closer to them. This is what my uncle did when he went back to Italy to be with his parents.

By this time, I was out of grammar school and had all summer to enjoy and wonder how high school would be like.

In 1938, I started to go to Benson Tech High School, which was a vocational school with a three- or four-year academic course. If you planned to go to college, you would take the four-year course. Benson Tech trained more journeymen for different trades than any other school in the USA. I took up the machine shop trade. I also played ball for Benson.

Times were very tough, and jobs were scarce. Some of my friends who I had played against at different parks and CYO, I ended up playing with on the same team in high school, or playing against them at the different high schools they went to.

During the summer, I delivered Rice Krispies samples for 25 cents per hour. My very good friend, John Gianninni, helped me get the job. At least fifty people had applied for the fifteen job openings. They would take us to Longview, Kalama, and Kelso, Washington to go door-to-door, ring the doorbell, and when the person answered, we would say, "Hello. This is a sample of Kellogg's Rice Krispies I have for you." The people were very happy to receive it. Sometimes we would get to work ten hours so we could make $2.50. I also delivered handbills for a grocery store and get fifty cents and three candy bars every week.

One of my friends had a 1926 Star Touring car with a canvas top and four of us decided to take a trip to Mexico in it. Paul Monfils, Joe Friedhoff, Bob Utter, and I had some yellow paint and painted our names on the doors. And in large letters, we painted "California or Bust."

We took Highway 99 and Coast Highway 101, making as many stops to 76 Service Stations as we could, to get their decals to put on our windshield. We averaged 25 to 35 miles per hour. Our first night was spent in Central Point, Oregon. We parked on a hill in case we could not start the car the next morning. This was better than pushing it. Our sleeping arrangements were two of us sleeping in the car and two on the ground, and we took turns on this. We always bought the least expensive gas, and at one service station, we bought poly gas for nine and nine-tenths cents per gallon. Generally, gas prices were around 17 to 22 cents per gallon.

We arrived in San Francisco and pulled into a park late at night. It was my turn to sleep in the car. In the middle of the night, we heard a loud roar and I was so frightened I thought I was going to go through the canvas roof. We did not know we had parked on the zoo's grounds.

The next night we stayed at the YMCA close to the waterfront. We paid 75 cents a night, and bought a cup of coffee and two doughnuts for fifteen cents. We went to see the San Francisco Fair on Treasure Island and had a great time. You could not miss our car because it stood out like a sore thumb, and when we got back to the car, a lot of people were looking at it and wondering what the screwballs who owned it looked like.

We left San Francisco and headed for Madera, where I was born. We visited my aunt and uncle, and my cousins Roy, Bill, and Gloria. Gloria got permission to use Roy's Plymouth convertible to drive us to Yosemite National Park. It was such a great treat for us to see this breathtaking place. While staying in Madera, we put up a tent for the night. The next day we headed for Los Angeles, and on the way, we had to drive up the Grapevine, which is very steep. We couldn't go over ten miles per hour. When we went downhill, we sped up to sixty miles per hour. We met the Oberti Olive family, which were good friends of my cousin, and got to see the cotton fields and great vineyards. We arrived in Tijuana, Mexico, and had a lot of fun looking around, but we were not able to buy anything even though all the merchandise were great bargains. The Mexican people were very nice to us and made us feel comfortable. We stayed there a few hours and then headed back to good old Oregon.

Whenever we stopped, many people wanted to take our picture and would give us fruit to eat. One day, when we came out of church, we saw a crowd had gathered and they were admiring our bright yellow car. This was the best and most enjoyable vacation I ever had while growing up. I will never forget the friends that went along on this trip. I had $28 when I started my trip, and when we arrived back in Portland, Oregon, I had about two dollars left. If I had known I was going to end up with that much, I would have spent a dollar in Tijuana, Mexico.

Portland had a doughnut shop called Sugar Crust. We'd buy day-old doughnuts for ten cents a dozen; three dozen for 25 cents.

The home of Paul and his brother Vernie "Curly" Monfils was always open for us to visit them. Curly was a great ball player and ready to start high school. The summer before high school started, Curly's idol—who was signed up to play for the Cleveland Indians Farm Team—was up at bat, and he swung at the ball. But the bat slipped out of his hand and it hit Curly in the eye. Curly was taken to the hospital but they could not save his eye. The other eye went blind and now he is totally blind. Curly lost one full year of school and started his high school at the Oregon Blind School in Salem, Oregon. I did not know him at this time. I had the pleasure of meeting him when he was on vacation at his home. He wrestled for the blind school and was an outstanding wrestler. He could play any instrument, including the piano. He was a genius.

After graduating from high school, Curly enrolled at Willamette University and was on their honor roll and wrestled for the university and was named a Northwest Wrestling Champion. He was a great golfer and he would shoot in the 48 to 55 for nine holes, being blind. He played golf only three or four times a year. He had been good enough to have been a great professional ball player. Curly weighed only 125 pounds and he could pin two of us down when we wrestled with him. He was really that great and I was lucky to be one of his friends.

This accident became a real tragedy for the batter. It ended up that he never did play for the Cleveland Indians. This bothered him so much that he ended up in a mental hospital.

**Vernie "Curly" Monfils with his seeing eye dog Cap.
The black car in the background in the right photo
is the 1926 Star Touring car we took to California and Mexico.**

Summer was over and we were ready to start another school year. I was very happy to get back to school and see some of my friends. When basketball season started, I would ride my bike. One night after basketball practice, it was raining very hard and on my way home a streetcar was going by and as it passed, a car was turning left and I landed on the hood of the car. The driver was so worried that I was hurt. I was not hurt, but I was in shock and my bike was damaged. My front wheel looked like a figure eight. The driver helped me straighten it out and kept asking me if I was okay. I assured him that I was. I got on my bike and headed for home. I never did tell my parents about my accident because I did not want them to worry about me.

We lived a little over two miles from where I went to high school and sometimes I would ride my bike or bum a ride. I did enjoy walking, rain or shine, but during basketball practice, I would ride my bike because it would be dark when practice was over. I'd pass the Bradley Bakery where you could buy day-old individual pies at two for five cents, which during those times was a terrific bargain. These pies were very good and tasty.

In downtown Portland was a place called the Coney Island Restaurant on SW Washington Street. You could buy a Coney Island hot dog loaded with onions and sauce for ten or fifteen cents. Portland had, and still has, some great outstanding restaurants.

The greatest hamburger you could buy was at Yaw's Top Notch Restaurant. Two brothers started in a small restaurant, then built a larger one and amassed a fortune. They ground their own hamburger. They were always packed and they made the best pies. I could not afford to go there very often. I can cook up a very good hamburger, but not as good as they did. Their wait staff was very good. The owners died off, and in short time there was no more Yaws. Older people who lived in Portland during the years Yaws Top Notch was in existence have told me how much they miss that restaurant, and so does my family. If there is perfection for a hamburger, they had it.

My favorite restaurants in Portland are Trader Vic's, The Ringside, Jake's Crawfish, Oregon Oyster House, and Country Kitchen. The California Bay Area restaurants I like best are the Fairmont Hotel, Trader Vic's, Spengers, Fior Di Italia, Fleur De Lis, and several good places on the pier. None of the owners of the restaurants that I just mentioned have any knowledge of what I am saying about them. But whenever I am in any area where these restaurants are located, I dine there.

We Are Now At War—December 1941

I really enjoyed going to Benson Tech and I was learning a trade. At that time, there were about 2,800 students, all boys, attending Benson. We were at school when we heard that Japan had bombed Pearl Harbor on December 7, 1941. There were a lot of students enrolled in the National Guard and many were pulled out of school. They ended up in the 41st Division. Schools and business buildings had their windows blacked out. I could not believe that we were in the state of war. This really gave me an odd feeling.

The defense plants were in full operation. When school was out, I went to Iron Fireman Manufacturing Company to apply for a job. They would not hire me because I was too young. I decided to go every day to apply for the job. I knew they would get tired of seeing me, and a little time later, they hired me. I was making sixty cents an hour and this was big money.

I purchased a 1932 Plymouth four-door for $150 and it was a very straight car in excellent condition. When school started again, I asked the foreman if I could get on the graveyard shift, and he let me get on his shift. This was only a six-and-a-half-hour shift and a lot of the machinists wanted to be on this shift. One of them asked why I got the chance for this shift. I said, because I asked to be on this shift. Sometimes you have to ask for what you want.

This graveyard shift gave me the time to go to school and to play ball. This really worked out very well for me, but after a few months, I was only half-awake in class, which was not helping me much. I was getting only four to five hours sleep each night. I hated to leave school, because I would lose out playing one more year of sports. I flunked my Chemistry class. I did not like Chemistry. I was afraid of it. I never did any homework for that class.

I did not finish high school, even though my parents wanted me to finish. I just kept working at Iron Fireman. Times were still tough and the steady job took priority. I did learn a lot at Iron Fireman working on all types of machines.

My sister went to Immaculata Academy High School and she had a friend who was thinking of not going to the prom because she did not want to go with the friend she had gone with the year before. My sister asked me if I might consider taking her friend to the prom. I asked my sister, *What does she look like?* and my sister said her picture was in the paper because she was in a play. I looked at the photo and told my sister I would go with her friend, even though I had already turned someone else down. I was going on a blind date.

I called Elaine Albert to meet her over the phone. She did have a very nice speaking voice. She set a time for me to pick her up. My dear friend Bob Rauch and his lovely girlfriend Violet Hunter went with us. I was not a great dancer, but Elaine really helped me along. After the prom, we went out to eat and had a great chicken dinner. I felt comfortable being with her, and after I took her home, I asked if I could call her and she said yes. We went on a date to Jantzen Beach Ballroom where the top bands of the land played, and then over to Jake's Crawfish to eat. Elaine loved the way they fried the crab legs. They have great food, and service second to none, with a relaxing atmosphere you do not want to miss.

I liked working at Iron Fireman but did not like working with the cutting oil, and decided to try to get a job with the railroad. I was hired, and then I went back to Iron Fireman to resign.

I went to work for the Northern Pacific Terminal as a fireman. We didn't get paid until we learned our job, which sure made us learn quickly. While working for the railroad, I helped shake down coal burners and prepared beds of coal for the locomotives that pulled passenger trains. This was really a fun job. My first job as a fireman on a switch engine was nerve-wracking. I fired for the strictest engineer, a man notorious for being hard to fire for. One day, we needed to pull forty boxcars and oil tank cars out to the lake yard. I had my fires set, oil pressure right, the steam gauge in order, and we were ready to pull. We barely got one hundred feet when I lost most of my steam. Black smoke was coming out of the stack and we had to stop. The engineer was angry with me because we had to build our steam pressure back up in order to continue to our destination. Later, as I learned my job a little better, I got the same engineer again and he was very nice and much easier to work for. Sometimes we would take a coal burning train to Union Station to hook onto the passenger cars. At the lake yard, we would make up trains by getting the boxcars, oil tankers, and lumber cars ready to go to different parts of the country.

I was still playing basketball when I was not working. I was on the extra board at work, which means they can call you anytime to report to work. When you are on the extra board, you would be with a different engineer most of the time. If you worked 15 hours and 55 minutes, they could call you back after ten hours of rest.

The yardmaster really treated all of us very nice and I always looked forward to going to work for this well-run railroad company. The engineer would teach you his job so that when you had the chance to be an engineer, you knew how to take over the job. Sometimes I would bring my lunch of a couple of cheese sandwiches. I'd put them on the engine boiler and have melted cheese sandwiches. Tillamook cheese is the best.

I decided to enlist in the service knowing that when I would be discharged, my job would be waiting for me upon my return. The railroad lines all worked on the seniority basis. When a new job would open, they would post it on the board and anyone could bid on it. Whoever had the most whiskers would get the job. Working on the railroad was the most fun job that I ever had, and it paid well. After you caught on, it was a very easy job.

My girlfriend, Elaine Albert, and I really got along very well. I had no intention of getting married until I was in my late thirties. But after knowing her for a while, I knew that if I did get married, it would be to a girl like her. I soon decided that I would like to get married at a younger age and so Elaine and I got engaged. Even though I changed the timetable, I knew I did not want to get married while I was in the service. My plan was that when I got out of the service, I wanted to put a down payment on a small house and make sure I had enough money for the first baby and, if it was a boy, I would have enough for a circumcision.

I enlisted in the maritime service, a branch of the Coast Guard. I was sent to Catalina Island for boot camp training. I wanted to get in the Steward's Department so I could get out to sea sooner. Catalina Island was so beautiful, and we had the opportunity to see great stars in person and great shows before we had to ship out. The Chicago Cubs had their spring training there. Every day, we would walk by Zane Grey's house, which was next to the water. The island was owned by the Wrigley Chewing Gum family. A lot of them come over to entertain us before we had to ship out. They had some of the greatest chefs there, and the food was excellent. I ate like a hungry horse.

I had selected enlistment in the maritime branch because it gave me a chance to learn a lot and great opportunities to advance to a higher position. The boot camp training did help me learn how to take care of myself in case my ship was sunk. I learned all about life saving. My machine shop training at Benson High School helped me get ahead in the service.

After leaving boot camp, I was sent to San Francisco for further orders. They bunked us up until we were assigned to a ship. My first ship was a lumber ship going up and down the Oregon coast. On the next ship, we made a couple of trips to the Hawaiian Islands to unload cargo. I realized I did not want to stay in the Steward's Department. I wanted to get in the Engine Department because I had been a fireman on the railroad. Any advancement that was made had to go through the Coast Guard and they gave you the exam and endorsement, if you passed. On my time off, I would go to the engine room to learn how to be an oiler, fireman, and water tender, and how to scrape the bearings and run the evaporators. I did pass my test, and did get my endorsements.

The next ship I was assigned to was heading out and we had no idea where we were going, but we did have bombs and all sorts of ammunition in our cargo. After two days at sea, we could see six other ships, and later we had a lot more ships with us, and we became a convoy. When we arrived at our destination, which was the Lingayen Gulf in the Philippines, we were out by ourselves unloading bombs and ammunition to the LSTs (Landing Ship Tanks) and other crafts. This was an invasion, and during this time, we had a lot of alerts because a lot of Japanese planes were flying overhead a few miles away. We would come up on deck to help man the guns. This happened a few times and when the alarm was clear, we would go back down to the engine room. After being down there for a little while, I heard a big, loud crash. A Japanese suicide plane had crashed into us. We went up on deck and could see the pilot's body scattered all over. We picked up some pieces of the plane. I kept one small piece of the plastic from the plane.

When we were hit, I had a scapular medal on that my mother found when I was twelve years old. She gave it to me and I never took it off. This little medal was about a third of the weight of a dime and when we got hit, this little medal dropped into my hands. While I was watching my steam gauges and very nervous, one of the armed guards on the ship made a heart out of my piece of plastic from the suicide plane and embossed the medal in it for me. I still have the heart and medal, which I gave to my wife. The only reason that we were all spared that day is because we had our booms out while we were unloading the bombs and ammunition to LST and other landing crafts. If not for the booms and God's help, I would not be here to tell you about it. I was very frightened when we had our general alarms. God was very generous to give us more time. It could have been the end for me.

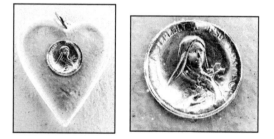

After the ordeal, we headed to Brisbane and Sydney, Australia, which is the second most beautiful harbor in the world next to Rio. Then we headed to Freemantle, a submarine base, then to Perth, which was a few miles away.

When we crossed the Equator, we had an initiation ceremony for everyone who had never crossed the Equator before. They filled one of the LSTs with water and each man got greased, painted, his hair cut, and then dunked into the water. The Captain of the ship went through this. He was a very good sport about it.

Leaving Perth, we headed to Geraldton, which has a very small pier. When we got ashore, a lot of people were there and they gave us a nice warm welcome. Some even invited us to their homes. The Australians are very nice people. I really loved Australia and the people there. I won three pounds on their National Lottery. The beer was very good, but they served it for only two hours at a time because it was scarce. We would queue up for our turn.

We had to take on food supplies before we left Australia. We then headed for Aden, Arabia, and took on bunkers and went through the Suez Canal, which was very exciting for me. From Suez, we went to Oran, North Africa, then to Bari, Italy. A lot of ships were sunk and scuttled in the harbor. I was hoping to get to northern Italy where my parents came from, but they were still fighting there.

While in Bari, I met some people and because I could speak Italian, they invited me to their house. I mentioned to the steward that I'd like to buy some meat to give to the people as a gift and he gave it to me. When I took the meat to this family, they could not believe their eyes. They were so happy because they rarely had a chance to buy meat during the war. I had a very nice time visiting with them, being able to converse with them in Italian. They lived in meager homes and did not have very much because the war was so hard on the people.

We loaded up a lot of prisoners of war to take back to the United States. They were treated very well and fed very well. They were happy to be war prisoners of our country since they were prisoners. It is too bad that other countries don't treat their prisoners as well as we do. These prisoners that we had on the ship were very happy that they were captured. Some of them could speak English and we did get a chance to talk to them. One prisoner of war told me he was happy that we had been captured.

My shore leave pass, Suez Canal.

While on the Mediterranean Sea, one of the crew was in serious condition and we were not able to care for him. We had to get help. We were tossed a line from a destroyer to secure a breeches buoy. A canvas seat in the form of breeches hung from a life buoy running on a hawser, which was used to haul persons from one ship to another ship. This was how we were able to get the seaman to the destroyer's hospital. This was the first time I witnessed such an operation, although I did see something similar using a life buoy in a movie once. The Mediterranean Sea was a little rough while this life-saving operation was going on. To see this with my own eyes was out of this world. We never did find out how the seaman fared.

On our way back to the States, I was not feeling well and had a hard time standing my watch. I could not hold down food and had no appetite. My face and body was a dark yellow color and I realized I was coming down with yellow jaundice. I went to the marine hospital in Maryland and they checked me out. Since I lived on the West Coast, they suggested I go to the marine hospital in Seattle, Washington. I was with two other crewmembers heading for the West Coast, and one of them, Bernie Hughes, decided to buy a used car and invited us to drive back there with him.

I smoked about two packs of cigarettes a year, but on our ship, I would get a carton every week. When I got off the ship, I gave the cartons to my friends because they were rationed in the US, like most everything was.

The gasoline was rationed and Bernie Hughes did not have any allotment for gas coupons. We had to stop many places to get some gas coupons as we travelled west. When we arrived in St. Louis, Missouri, we went to the main office and told them that we could not get enough gas coupons unless we made a lot of stops before we arrived home. The one stop at St. Louis they gave us enough gas to get home and much more. That got rid of a big headache for us. We were then on our way home without the worry of getting any gas coupons.

I was able to get into the marine hospital in Seattle, but after a few days of recuperating, I became very bored, so I asked my doctor if I could leave the hospital. The doctor said that the only way I could leave would be against medical advice and I would have to sign a release form. I was so happy that I gave the doctor two bottles of whiskey that came from rations. The doctor put me on a strict diet of eggs and salads. I ate a dozen eggs every day for six months. I stayed on the strict diet and got back to good health and was able to return to the service.

Left to right: My pals Ed Finley, Frank Antonacci, me, and Bob Rauch, 1945.
We were all home on leave at the same time even though we were in
different branches of the service.

On one of my trips, we docked at a pier on the San Francisco waterfront. We had a black cook and we were at the end of the trip. He had a lot of luggage to take down the gangplank, so I picked up two of his suitcases and took them down for him. When I got back on the ship, two sailors said, "You helped that black fellow." And I said I would even help them. I really could not believe what I was hearing. They must have been raised by the wrong parents.

When I was on leave in Portland, Oregon, I took my fiancée Elaine to Jantzen Beach Park for an outing. We took the trolley bus to the park and had a very nice time. When we left to go back to her parents' house, a few young and old people were riding on the trolley. Then two sailors with their girlfriends got on and they sat in the back and our seat was in front of them. After the bus started to move along, the sailors and their girlfriends started to talk loud and swear. I turned around in a polite way and asked them not to swear. A couple of minutes later they started up again and they said no one was going to tell them what to do.

One more time I asked them in a nice way to stop the vulgar talk, and one of the sailors stood and said, "What are you going to do about it?" I said I would throw them off the bus. He grabbed me and I got a headlock on him and had him on the steps of the rear exit. I told the bus driver to stop the bus and open the rear door, then I pushed the sailor off the bus and told the other sailor and the two girls to get off, too. When they were all off the bus and on the sidewalk, they gave me the finger and then they hollered back that they would get me. The passengers clapped for me. I told the bus driver it was his job to do what I did. I have never been in a fight and this was the closest I had ever gotten to being in one.

When you think enough of a woman and would like to marry her, it is so important to talk things over before you actually wed. Talk about your likes and dislikes, how many children you would like to have, habits you both have. This is critical. Be courteous to each other before and after you get married. If you can't make decisions together today, you will not be able to do so later.

The woman has the upper hand and should use it. She has control if the man thinks enough of her. He will open the door for her, and walk on the outside of the sidewalk to give her protection. If a woman does not get this type of respect, she should dump the guy. If a woman does get tied up with him, she will regret it all the time she has to live with her mistake. The bed is not the only part of a woman's relationship. She needs to have a good companionship. The man and woman must have respect for each other. This will cement their happiness and result in a happy marriage.

Before you get married, make sure you know the background of the person that you plan to marry. Don't hurry it up. Make sure you want this person as your mate. You must look forward to life because time goes by very fast and this is why it is so important to try and make the right decisions. Nothing is perfect, but you can get closer if you think about your choices. If you have a problem, you must discuss it together. Never go to bed in anger. Straighten it out now or you will start to drift away from each other. A marriage is two-fold. Respect each other and you will have a better life companion. You have to take the bitter with the sweet. You must be strong. Try not to argue. Do not just consider only yourself. Consider that the children you bring into this world all need the love and attention they deserve. Remember, you will get old soon and at least let the children grow up and earn their own respect. With your good guidance, they will turn out to be happy with no hang-ups. Children learn most of their habits from their parents.

Never hit your kids in the head or on their back, or slap them in the face. Do not ever talk your children down in front of anyone or make fun of them or embarrass them. Do not run down anyone because of his or her color, race, or religion, especially in your home. This is where hate is taught. Parents should never swear at their children or at each other.

While Elaine and I were dating, we discussed these beliefs and we would question each other on our likes and dislikes. This helped us and will help you appreciate each other more. There should be no secrets between you and your spouse before you get married.

There are things a woman should think about before marriage. Is the man courteous to you? Does he run you down? Does he lose his temper or swear a lot? Does he drink a lot or do drugs? Does he get along with his parents and does he want a family? Does he have a job? How many jobs has he had in the last three years? And why did he change jobs so often? Are your religious beliefs compatible? If you want him to join your church and he says he will do it after you are married, know that it will never happen. If it is not good enough before marriage, it won't change later. The honeymoon will be over very soon and you need to get these things sorted out early. The honeymoon can last the full life of your marriage, but you have to practice and work together. You will have your ups and downs, but you must work things out in a civil manner. Be patient before you make up your mind to get married.

Also, remember that the man has the right to know the same things about you. When you are going together and don't have any hang-ups, you will have an easier time talking things out and can appreciate each other more.

Don't try to achieve everything at once; take one step at a time. If one of you has a business idea, you should try to explore it. To have a goal in life and not achieve it is not a sin, but not having a goal at all is a sin. You cannot believe how much energy you will have when you keep a positive attitude and always try to better yourself and your family. Just about everything is possible. When one door closes, there will be another one opening. Have faith, which will guide and help you get to where you want to go. Maybe you have heard the old expression about "waiting for their ship to come in." If you don't send one out, none will come in. Don't make excuses for yourself.

Marriage is a two-fold union and couples need to remember this before considering divorce. You never get good at anything unless you keep trying. The more you try, the better you will do.

I have a very happy life sentence with my wife, Elaine. You can have your marriage as pleasant as you want it to be... "It takes two to do it." A marriage is a new way of life for the wife and the husband. You have to have tolerance or learn to develop tolerance.

During your engagement period, you will have time to learn more about your spouse. You will find out if your spouse-to-be is a phony, or a stand-up person. Getting married is a very serious commitment and if either of you have hang-ups, you need to get them out of the way or they will haunt you throughout your marriage. I know people who were not happy in their marriage and as the years passed, they both became grouchy old people. That attitude is a real waste of their lives.

People now seem too reckless with their lives—jumping from one person to another, not knowing anything about the person they shack up with. They might be carrying a social disease, or might get pregnant. Really, you must think about it—is it worth it to shatter your life, and maybe become a parent too soon?

Elaine and I with Frank Antonacci and Mary Erceg, at our wedding.

Elaine and I were married on September 14, 1944.

We Are Getting Married!

Elaine and I were married September 14, 1944 at Blessed Sacrament Catholic Church in Portland, Oregon. One of Elaine's very close friends, Mary Erceg, was her maid of honor, and my dear friend, Frank Antonacci, was my best man. I was home on leave and we spent our honeymoon at Rockaway Beach, on the Oregon coast. We did not know any of the motels there, so I called information to get a phone number of a motel where we could stay. The information operator could not provide any details other than phone numbers. So I asked her to mention the names of some motels. Of all the names she mentioned, Our Haven sounded good, so we made a reservation there. It was the worst of all of them. We were not that fussy and we really enjoyed our honeymoon, so that is all that matters.

I really lucked out in having a great mother-in-law and father-in-law, and great brothers-in-law Joseph, Frank, and Robert Albert.

The house we purchased was fifty years old, perhaps older. If you placed a marble on the kitchen floor, it would roll into the living room. We bought used furniture, and repaired, then papered a room for a child that we hoped to have. This was wartime. I was so happy we had this little old house because my wife would not have to worry or deal with a landlord while I was overseas.

While I was still on leave and had to go downtown to do some business, I ran into one of the crewmen. He showed me that he had his electrician endorsement. I was very happy for him and I said to myself that if he could get the endorsement, I should be able to do the same. When I arrived home, I told my wife about the crewman getting his electrician endorsement and that I was going to try and get the same endorsement. I bought some books on electricity and really studied hard, and with Elaine's help, decided to take the Coast Guard's exam. I did take the exam and passed. I was then qualified to go on a ship as a chief electrician, or a second electrician.

Outside our house at Northeast 14th Street & Alberta in Portland, Oregon.

I was aware enough not to go on a ship as a chief electrician, knowing I would do better as an assistant. I really did not want to work with electricity because I was afraid of it. I was assigned to a ship and I met the chief electrician and told him I was naïve about electricity, but that I could do all the labor needed. He said I was the person he wanted. I was there anytime he needed me, and I worked hard. I also got the chance to learn more about the ship's electrical system. From that, I started to understand, and like, electricity.

The chief electrician and I got along very nice and I had a lot of fun working with him. He was thirty years older than I was. Later down the road, I heard about the shipmate who had told me he received his electrician endorsement. I found out he was some kind of a genius in science. If I had known that sooner, I may not have taken the test or tried to get this endorsement. My grammar school teacher, Sister Mary Margaret, had told me to always have a positive attitude and to be a good listener. I've never forgotten.

I was assigned to the Mankato Victory ship for a shakedown cruise on the Columbia River, which flows into the Pacific Ocean. The crew was late getting to the ship. But as we got close, we noticed that the ship was in flames. A welding hose had caused the fire. This was the one time being late saved a close call on my life.

One ship I was on went through the Panama Canal. This was such a great endeavor and such a great work of engineering that it is hard to believe how it was accomplished. I really enjoyed this great feat. I was a Junior Assistant Engineer on that ship.

Finally, the war came to an end and I decided to go back to the job waiting for me at the railroad in Portland. It was nice to see the old faces that I hadn't seen since I entered the service.

Elaine and I purchased a piece of property we planned to build a three-plex on. We went to see Benjamin Franklin Savings and Loan to see if they might finance our project. We talked to Bob Hazen, the owner's son. We had a title of survey, a lot that was free and clear, and building plans that had already received city approval. Hazen had told us to gather all this together and said when we did, he would give us the loan. But when we went back to complete the final bank paperwork, Bob Hazen said they could not give us the loan because Portland would not be growing that much.

He was very negative, and I told him that all of us coming out of the service will be getting married and having families, which will force Portland to grow without anybody coming in from the outside. He still turned us down.

However, when we were getting our building plan approved, the person checking our plan told us that if we made the walls two inches wider, we could someday sell the units as condos. Each unit had its own utilities and basement. We had a firm bid to build our three-plex for just under $17,000. We had $3,000 down and needed only a $14,000 loan. We were allowed to charge a total of $297 for the three units because of the OPA (Office of Price Administration) Price Board. We figured we could have sold them for at least $35,000, regardless of what Bob Hazen said. We had already sold our first house, which is why we had the money to do our project. This was in 1946. My wife and I were 22 years old and I think our age might have played a part in being turned down by Bob Hazen.

When my wife and I were going together, we had talked about building a school for underprivileged children. We knew that if we could build the three-plex, we could sell it for a very good profit. We wanted to parlay this so someday we could start our school.

I was still working at the railroad and selling photo mounts to the photography studios in my spare time. I always looked at the classified ads and I read an ad stating that someone wanted a business partner. I called to meet with the person, and we did end up as partners in a photography studio. We were located in the Selling Hirsh Building on Park and Washington streets in downtown Portland. The studio did not produce too much money, and after a few months, we started to talk about buying a restaurant. I was still working for the railroad.

The restaurant that caught our eye was located at the east end of the Burnside Bridge. The Bridgeport Hotel was next to us and below our restaurant were the Meadowland Dairy and Ice Cream Factory. Across the street were the Multnomah County Sheriff's Department Motor Pool, and Lily Ice Cream Cone Co. The Hills Brothers Coffee Co. office was in the Bridgeport Hotel, and Fishel Awning Co. was across the street.

Before we moved into our restaurant, we tore out just about everything in the restaurant so we could redo the dining area. We did it all in knotty pine, and when we finished the remodeling it really looked very nice. We hired a chef who had worked in some very nice restaurants in Portland. We had pinball machines, punchboards, and a very large back room with slot machines. We wanted to convert the back room into a businessmen's social club. We had the ideal location because there were no schools, churches, or playgrounds within a mile.

We built up a nice business and had a nice, steady crowd coming in to eat. The fellow that was in charge of taking care of the Sheriff's cars liked to play the punch boards, and one day, while he was playing, the waitress came to me to say that he had a lot of the punches on the floor. I asked her if he was winning a lot, and she said no. I told her that when he starts winning, ask him if he wants to pay for the ones that fell on the floor.

The Sheriff's deputies, after they got off work, would come in our back room to drink and play the machines. We did have a beer and wine license. During this time, nightclubs could not sell you a drink over the bar. You had to take your bottle and check it in. Then the bartender would mix you a drink and you would pay for it, and if you wanted to leave, you would take your bottle home. The steady customers would check their bottle in and leave it until their next visit. If you were just visiting and did not have a bottle, you could still get a drink. They would just use a friend's bottle.

My first restaurant on the east end of the Burnside Bridge—on the ramp.
I was 22 years old.

One night when I was cooking, three Mayflower truck drivers
came in to eat. They ordered three T-bone steaks. After I served
them, they called me over to their booth and told me that the steaks
were not good. I apologized and cooked up three more steaks. They
complained again, and I threw the six steaks into the garbage can. I
asked them if I could try again; I felt so bad and defeated. They told
me to go ahead and I cooked up three more steaks. They called me
back to their booth and told me that all the steaks had been good,
but they had a bet going that they could make me angry. My wife
was in the restaurant waiting for me. They paid for all nine steaks
and gave my wife a ten-dollar tip. They mentioned they did this a
lot, and enjoyed doing it.

The Rose Festival Parade route crossed the Burnside Bridge from downtown and passed right in front of our restaurant. We knew this was going to be our best business day of the year. We purchased eight hundred hot dogs, three hundred bottles of beer, sandwiches, coffee, soft drinks, and lunch fixings. The chef said that I bought too many supplies.

One hour before the parade started, we did not have much business, and the chef seemed to be correct in his opinion. We were hustling on the bridge to sell hot dogs and sandwiches. All of a sudden, the restaurant was packed and we were selling like mad. When the day ended, we had only a couple dozen beers left, a few hot dogs, and a half dozen sandwiches left. We took in a couple thousand dollars, which was a lot of money for the one day. The chef was upset because we did so well. He should have been happy since we were on the same team. Some chefs think they are like little tin gods. The chef was angry with me because I told him to wash the lettuce before it was served. He decided to leave the job and I hated to see him go. He was really a nice guy, but with a short fuse.

I had a great desire to have my spaghetti sauce and pasta products canned. I went to a custom cannery in Portland and explained to the owner what I wanted to do. He told me to get my spaghetti sauce and pasta all made up and he would put it into cans and cook it all again to kill the bacteria. It really tasted good, but I would not put it on the market. I later found out that the canner gave me the wrong information about how it should have been done. I had to give up the idea that I was going to put both Franco American Spaghetti and Chef Boyardee, out of business. I really thought I could do it. They are still here and my product went by the wayside. I still want to have my product on the market, but it would need to be frozen.

The Japanese Internment Camps

I felt our country did a terrible ordeal in putting the Japanese people in the internment camps. This should not have happened. Their property was stolen from them, that they worked so hard to own. They should have put Germans and Italians in these camps as long as they took it out on the Japanese citizens. I got along very well with the Japanese.

We had many Japanese students at Benson Tech where I went to school. They were very nice and easy-going. Many of them were on the honor roll. I felt so sorry for them when they were put into the camps because they did not deserve this type of treatment. They were very good citizens. A lot of people made a lot of money because of their loss. They should be ashamed of themselves. What they should have done was to put a freeze on the Japanese people's assets and property. That way, they would get their belongings back when the war was over. The compensation that some received was peanuts. They were just as good citizens as we are, or better. I trusted them very much and always have.

What they did to some Italians and Germans is put them on a curfew. If Germany ever did this on our soil, you would have had a lot of bund members coming out of hiding because they were very strong in wanting to take over our country. If the time was right, they would be ready in a heartbeat. There were bund meetings all over the state of Oregon. All of us that are lucky enough to live in the best country in the world should concentrate on respecting our country and teaching our children to respect it and become good citizens. Your own home is the best classroom to do this. We all learn a lot by listening to others giving their two cents worth of opinions, but do not be swayed by others—your opinion might be as good, or better, than their opinion. You must be your own person, and this will give you a better chance to make more sound evaluations situations.

I resigned from the railroad to devote more time to our restaurant. One of our steady customers was the manager for Hal Hillman Studebaker Company. He repeatedly tried to get me to become a car salesman for him, but I always put him off. I was hoping to get a businessmen's social club started. Portland really needed something like this; it was one of the most wide-open cities in the United States.

Eventually, I did get the opportunity to open a social club, as long as I agreed to take in a partner. But the prospective partner was not a person I wanted to have around me and I did not trust him. I am the only person I rely on when it comes to choosing a business partner. I passed on the offer in a nice way so that nobody had bad feelings.

A week after I turned down that offer, while I still owned the restaurant on the east end of the Burnside Bridge near Portland's downtown area, someone won over a hundred dollars on the pinball machine. I was not there at the time. My restaurant partner was there. I had told him that if someone wins over ten dollars on the pinball machine, have them come back the following day to collect their winnings. He told me the winner had already been paid off. I did not get angry with him. He was old enough to be my father and a real nice person. Getting angry does not get your money back. So just grin and bear it. The person who had won the hundred dollars used a wire to run up the games.

One hundred dollars was a lot of money, especially when you could buy a large piece of ham, eggs, hash browns, and toast for 65 cents, and your coffee was ten cents, with refills. Lunch was 45 cents. A T-bone steak was $1.75, and that came with a salad and all of the trimmings. We served the best food, or as good as the best that you could eat in Portland. This is a fact. I could have had many places to operate if I would have given certain people side money. I would not give one cent to anybody that was involved. The people that wanted to deal with me were bums with a lot of money and with no sense. I really did not want this type of person around me. This is why it is wise for everyone to have a mind of their own. Never sell yourself short. Pick your own friends and you will be much happier with your life.

I really love the restaurant business where you meet some very nice people as they come into your life. I was in my early twenties and I decided to talk to my partner about selling our restaurant, and he went along with my idea. We did sell the restaurant.

I decided to drive a taxicab for Union Cab Company, which turned out to be a great experience that opened my eyes. My parents had taught me to be a gentleman always, and this did help me when driving a cab. I would always open the door for my customers and give them my card and ask them to call me when they needed a cab the next time. This did get me a lot of business and some very good tips.

I got a lot of business from the ladies of the evening and treated them with the same respect I show to all ladies. They told me the reason they called me when they needed a cab was because I was very courteous to them. Some of these ladies lived in the most exclusive areas of Portland. I really received some very good tips from them. I had a good business going, and was thinking of buying my own taxicab.

One night, two fellows got into my cab and wanted me to drive them to the Benson Hotel. When I was just about there, they asked me if I knew where they could get a bottle of booze. This hit me with a funny feeling, and I told them that I knew someone who might have a bottle for them, but it was way out of town in the St. John's area. They told me to go ahead, and I was on my way to St. John's. When I arrived there, I stopped at a house and told my passengers I would check if the party was home. I got back in the cab and told them that the party was not home, but I have another place that might be open, and they said, "Okay. Take us there." I did this three different times and my meter was really clicking very fast. And after all of this, they decided to head back to town. This was a very costly fare. My gut feeling was very much on the money. On the way back, I asked them if they wanted to go the Benson Hotel and they said, "Drop us off where we got in." When I stopped, two fellows approached the car and when the door opened, they said, "Did you get him?" I would never sell liquor to anyone. They did not know it, but I was playing cat and mouse with them. I let other cab drivers know what they were trying to do to me and if they did sell any liquor, they had better be careful. The two agents in my cab never gave me a tip.

Driving a cab, you do not have to sell anything illegal to make real good money. I always got good tips driving a cab. I have to admit that I really enjoyed driving a taxi, but I decided to quit. While driving a taxicab, I learned a lot about people. It's an experience you wouldn't want to miss, if you ever get the chance to drive a cab.

Starting My Career In The Car Business

I went over to see Bill Engel, a restaurant customer who had wanted me to sell autos for him. He hired me. We worked out of the used car lot located on Grand Avenue at Burnside, on the east side of town. I was paid only when I sold trucks.

We had some people come on the lot and I was told to go talk to them because no one else wanted to talk to the people. They looked dirty. I greeted them, and after talking to them for a while, I found out that they worked on a farm. They asked me if I could come out to the farm to show them the truck because they had to get back to work right away.

The next day I went out to see them and they ended up buying the truck. When I got back, everyone was amazed that I had made the sale and that the men had paid cash for the truck. It turned out the men were very nice, hard-working people. They gave me a prospect and I made another sale to their friends.

The general manager and the truck manager wanted to teach me how to sell the fleet accounts, so they took me to a transfer and trucking company to learn the ropes. When we arrived at the place, I noticed that across the street were two old flatbed trucks. I pointed them out to my manager, who laughed. He said every car dealer in town had tried to sell new trucks to the owner, who was in the used box and crate business. I asked if I could go over and talk to him. He laughed again and told me to give it a try. I went across the street to meet the owner.

The owner's name turned out to be Mr. Knowles. He was quite old. He introduced me to his lovely wife, and she was charming. I could sense that this would take a kid glove approach. I would not try and sell them anything. I just wanted to have a nice conversation with them.

In talking to Mr. Knowles, I found out he liked 1886 cigars and his wife liked chocolates. I explained why it would be a good idea to have a new unit, and he told me he'd already turned down every truck salesman trying to sell them a truck. He and his wife were very impressed in how I talked to them, especially in bringing his wife into the picture. When I was leaving, I asked if I could meet with him and his wife again. I ended up selling them a long flatbed truck and had his name put on each door. I sold them a little half-ton pickup too. I bought his wife a box of Van Duyn chocolates and a box of 1886 cigars for him. I would see him downtown where some of the vegetable and fruit stands were, and he was so proud of his truck. Later, he bought a new car from me and even helped me sell another truck to one of his friends.

I would go as far as 25 miles to prospect for customers. I did sell many trucks this way. I was proud of all my sales, but my proudest moment was when I went to the garbage dump to try to sell a Studebaker truck to the owners who were driving GMC, Reos, Fords, and Dodge trucks.

When I went to the dump, I would put the truck's hood up, open the cab doors, and then walk to the restaurant next door for coffee. It was called the BlowFly Inn (a very appropriate name). The garbage collectors owned their own trucks and business. They all laughed when I wanted to show them the Studebaker truck. Most of their trucks were heavy-duty units and I had to figure out the best approach to get their interest.

Our used car lot was located on Grand Avenue and Burnside

Street. It occupied a quarter of a block. The other three-quarters of the block was occupied by the Joe Fisher car lot. He was the largest Plymouth dealer in Oregon, put a lot of effort into advertising, and brought in many customers.

We did not have a large sign. In fact, it was so small that it was hard to see it. The manager wanted to have a large sign with our name on it. I told him that most of the people that came onto our lot thought we were part of Joe Fisher's dealership. Later, they got wise and put a high cement block divider between us and it blocked us out from his car lot. We liked it better the way it had been.

At that time, garbage collectors had to lift the garbage cans and dump them into the garbage box, which could cause soreness to their backs. After three trips to the dump, I finally got one of the truck owners to show a little interest. I told him I would like to include his wife in the discussion because it would be in his and his family's interest. I made an appointment to meet with them. Their home was on the upper end and they owned the best of cars.

I explained that I wanted to include the wife and family because I wanted to point out the health advantages of our truck. I said our truck was four inches lower than his current truck. This meant less chance of straining his back when lifting and emptying the garbage cans. It is the last inch or two that cause most strains. Also, he would get three to four more miles per gallon of gas and the running boards were inside the cab.

I sold them a truck, and they helped me sell two more trucks. When you sell trucks, you do have to know your competition and how to attack them. This really becomes a fun game. You have to hone yourself to become a professional salesman. We were really doing a great job and selling a lot of cars and trucks.

Hal Hillman Motors

SALES " **STUDEBAKER** " SERVICE

TELEPHONE GARFIELD 1241

4034 N. E. Broadway, Portland 13, Oregon

THE STUDEBAKER CORPORATION OF AMERICA--SOUTH BEND, INDIANA

SALES DEPARTMENT LETTER TO DEALERS   SALES DEPARTMENT

Subject:::CARRYING THE FIGHT TO THE ENEMY   DATE:: MARCH 24, 1931

I have been assigned the job of selecting a squad of champion dealers and sales managers - who can put over a championship job of selling in 1931.

You may think that's a tough assignment for a football coach -- I know it is. Mr. Cleary and Mr. Hoffman believe, however, that there is a close analogy between coaching a football team and directing a sales organization and from what I have learned during two seasons of traveling around among Studebaker dealers I am convinced I can help.

From my twenty years experience in football I am convinced that the way to win football games is to carry the fight to the enemy --- -- to play the game in their territory. In the season of 1928 we played defensive football - we let the other fellow carry the fight to us and as a result we lost four games. We profited by this mistake. The last two seasons we played offensive football. I know that this aggressiveness was very largely responsible for our success. What I have in mind now is developing a team of offensive dealers and sales managers who will play the game in the enemy's territory.

I am starting right now to develop my first string and if you want to be among them here is your chance.

First of all I want to be sure I have the material.. If you think this is going to be just a little by-play and perhaps you will string along, toss this in the wastebasket now; you are wasting your time. There isn't going to be room on my squad for all of you and I suggest that you make up your mind right now whether you are out for a place on the team or a seat on the bench..

If you think you already know all there is about sales management; if you are one of the type that starts out with a loud whoop and poop-lah the first day and then slow down to a walk when the going gets tough; if you think this is going to be a Deluxe excursoin with attendant banquets, wassail and paper hats - forget all about me. You had better spend your evening listening to Rudy Vallee. You won't fit into the Rockne System.

If, on the other hand, you are willing to get right down to earth and dig; if you have the character to drive yourself into mastering new ideas and putting them into play; if you are willing to start early in the morning and work until late at night if need be, injecting new life into your salesmen - then send your entry to me.

Hal Hillman Motors

SALES " STUDEBAKER " SERVICE

TELEPHONE GARFIELD 1241

4034 N. E. Broadway, Portland 13, Oregon

PAGE #2

I want to see every Studebaker dealer and sales manager out for the team. But I can't use any laggards who are satisfied with mediocre work. Better a few real men of championship caliber than a raft of candidates who will be satisfied if they make the scrub team.

Your first assignment will be sent you just as soon as you indicate that you are earnestly interested - that you are the kind of man we can depend on through the thick and thin of the coming battle. And the assignment will be a tough one.. If you make good, others will follow - and they will be still tougher. For ninety days they will keep coming, at intervals, and some of you will fall by the wayside in the course of events. But, in the final squad, we will have real championship material - capable of an All-American sales title.

Be on time. All applications mailed after midnight, March 31, will be carefully filed in the wastebasket.

LET'S GO!!!!

Knute K. Rockne

Sales Promotion Manager
Studebaker Corporation
South Bend, Indiana

P. S. Where a distributor or dealer employs a sales manager and both want to try for the team -- come ahead!!!

1931 BELONGS TO STUDEBAKER !

THE PROFIT FROM 29% OF GROUP "A" BELONGS TO YOU !

This letter from Knute K. Rockne, Coach of Notre Dame, really inspired me to sell Studebaker cars and trucks.

Mr. Hal Hillman, owner of the Studebaker dealership, passed away and the factory took the franchise away from the family. The business was shut down and we were all out of a job. This was a practice that all auto manufacturers had in their dealer franchise agreements. So I went to the Logan Oldsmobile dealership and was hired to work on the used car lot with my friend Ray Davidoff, who had previously been working with me at the Studebaker dealership. We sold a lot of cars. The dealership was like a country club. We were paid very well, plus received a bonus every three months, and a golf party at the Portland Golf and Country Club.

Nothing seemed to please Mr. Logan more than watching his salesmen and managers get totally drunk and then talking about it at the next sales meeting. He was a very short man, and when we attended sales meetings, he would sit in a chair that made him higher than us.

The shop repairing area was as clean as any showroom. Every Saturday and Sunday, a black American would come in to get the repair shop floor looking as nice as you would want in your house. Mr. Logan would go down there to watch the janitor work and talk to him, sharing some of his problems. The janitor was a very hard worker and put in all the hours he could because he wanted his children to have a college education. He and I had become good friends and occasionally he shared some of his frustrations with me. One day he told me that once, when Mr. Logan was telling him a sad story, he wanted to give Mr. Logan some money because he felt sorry for him. But Mr. Logan was a millionaire and then some.

Every year, by December 31, Mr. Logan wanted all used cars sold so he could start the new year with no inventory. We all thought he was a little odd, but he really was a very nice person.

Hershel McGriff, who won the Mexican Road Race, bought his Olds '88 from our dealership.

One day a man and a woman walked on our lot and decided on a car they wanted to buy. Ray and I took them to the sales office and started to write them up, but they said they had a car they were trying out. It turns out the car they were trying out was the same model and year as ours. I asked them which they liked the best, and they said ours. I asked his wife to sit tight while her husband returned the other car to where they had picked it up and I would follow him and bring him back to complete our transaction. We had to wait for our credit approval for the buyers.

The finance company called us back to ask us how much do the customers need. We told them that enough to pay for the car is what we needed. The finance company wanted to know how much more money did they want, because they would give them as much as $50,000. I told the finance company to quit kidding us, and they asked me if I really knew who they were, and I said no. They told us that she was one of the heiresses to the Corning Corporation and he was Frank Keaton, the son or grandson of Buster Keaton. After the sale was completed, which was my main concern, we had a chance to visit with our customers. They told us that her parents bought them a $52,000 house up in Portland Heights. They never bragged or let us know they had great wealth. They were very nice kids. Over the years, they bought a lot of cars from Ray and me.

One of the toughest customers came in on one of the hottest days ever in Portland. The customer was dickering for $25 that we needed to make our sale. It took us five hours to finally make the sale. The customer owned the Original Pancake House, a restaurant that is still at the same location today on SW 24th Street and SW Barbur Boulevard. The owner did buy us a couple of breakfasts.

My wife and I had been trying to have children ever since we got married. We had no success and started talking about adopting children. I was telling a fellow salesman about our problem and he told me that someone in his family had the same problem and visited Dr. Carl D. Heller, who helped them have children. This was the best news that I could hear.

I made an appointment to see Dr. Carl D. Heller. My wife had a lady doctor by the name of Dr. Elizabeth Helene Schirmer, and she made an appointment to see her. But before we went on our appointments, we discussed the fact that the problem might be with both of us, or just one of us. Regardless, if we could not have a child, we were going through with the adoption procedure.

Because I'd had yellow jaundice, my sperm count was very low. I had to take shots of pregnant mare serum in my rear cheeks every day. I would go to the doctor's office to discharge some sperm because they could not get a true potency unless it was done within ten minutes after discharge. I did this for three or more months. My wife needed to know when she ovulated, so I would take my wife's temperature every night and log it in each time. We started to have a great hope, with God's help.

While I was still working at Logan's, a fellow who had been driving a cab with me came by to visit. He showed me the paycheck he had received from the Ford dealership where he was then working. This was a nice hunk of money. I said, "That's very good for a monthly check," and he said that it was a two-week check. I told him that the Ford dealership was where I wanted to work.

The people who owned the Ford dealership owned a few other dealerships out of state. This company gave their employees the opportunity to better themselves and to advance to higher positions as long as they had the desire to work hard and smart. They did not care what your religion or race was; all they wanted you to do is make a lot of money selling cars.

I did get hired and asked to work on the used car lot, which was my preference. If I saw someone waiting for a bus in front of our dealership, I would give them my card and get their phone number, if possible. Even if a customer did not want to buy, I would call and see if maybe one of their friends might need a car. After I was there for a while, one of the salesmen asked me if I had met the owners of the Ford dealership, and I told him no, but they sure know who I am. He asked me why I thought that, and I said that they look at everyone's standings and I am in the top three every month. The biggest mistake that salesmen make is that they do not follow up and call their customers back to find out if they're happy with their purchase. That is the time to ask them for leads.

The dealership set up a clothing contest every month and I won a lot of great clothes. The company also set up a terrific contest where the winner and his wife would be sent on a tour through the Ford factory in Detroit. They set up strict rules for the contest. You had to do everything yourself with no help from anyone else. You had to make cold phone calls, send out postcards, put offers on windshields that said, If I could allow you 'X' amount of dollars on your car, would you consider buying a car or truck from me? And, of course, sell the most cars.

I knew I had to work real hard and be extra smart to win. I led all the way through the contest and found out that my runner-up had his wife doing some of his phone calls. This was a no-no. The way I found out was that I received a misdirected phone call by accident. The caller mentioned that my wife called him about buying a car from her husband. I asked him the name of the person he was calling, and he said he was calling for Bob Action. I told him that I was not Bob Action but I would transfer the call to him. I worked very hard to win and I put in real long hours throughout the contest. The last day of the contest, I left work at around 7 p.m. When I arrived home, I mentioned that we should go to Mac Barbecue in Milwaukie, Oregon, a small town next door to

Portland. On the way to Mac's, I told my wife that I won the contest, but knew I would get cheated out of it the next morning. I told her I would end up being the runner-up.

The next morning during our sales meeting, they announced the winner of the contest, Bob Action. I congratulated him and went over to the used car lot, and this is when I felt really defeated. I am my own person and not one to complain. I did a lot of thinking, and when I had my full composure, I told my friend and partner on the used car lot, Ray Davidoff, that if the company did not rectify the results of the contest the next day, I no longer wanted to work for them anymore because of the tactics they used.

I know that Bud Meadows and Mike Salta went out to dinner with Bob Action and their wives. I only told Ray Davidoff about my plans. Three hours went by and the owner was in town, and he came over to the used car lot and shook my hand and told me that he knew how hard I worked and that he was grateful. He announced that Bob and I, with our spouses, were going to get to go to Detroit to go through the Ford Factory and we had the choice to fly or take the train. They flew and my wife and I took the train.

The train ride was very exciting. When we arrived in Detroit, we got together with Bob and his wife for dinner. The next day we went through the factory, which was very enlightening. While we were still in Detroit, Bob received a call that his father passed away and this cut his trip short. Elaine and I picked up a new Ford Crown Victoria to drive back to Portland, Oregon.

One of Elaine's friends, Ruth Brule, who she'd gone to high school with (her married name is Ruth Stransz), lived in Clinton, Michigan. We stayed at their house with her and her husband for a couple of days. This gave Elaine a chance to visit with her friend.

Heading back home, we stopped in St. Louis, Missouri, and visited a friend of Elaine's sister, who lived across the street from us in Portland. We had a great time with them, and the next day we were on the road again heading to Reno, Nevada. When we arrived in Reno, we played the slot machines at Harold's Club. Something odd happened. We left as the winners of $38 after paying for our food and lodging.

Back on the road again, we headed for my birthplace, Madera, California, and to visit my relatives. We stayed with my cousin Gloria and Angelo Mazzetti. We visited with them, then went around visiting some of my other relatives.

After leaving Madera, we headed back to good old Portland. This trip was the greatest time of our life. The best thing that happened was that Elaine thought she might be pregnant. When we arrived home, she made an appointment to see her doctor. The doctor made the test and it showed negative, which was a real disappointment to us. I asked the doctor if it could have been misread, because my wife was crying. They took another reading and it came back positive and she shed no more tears. She was so happy to be pregnant after trying for years to be able to bear a child.

While I was still working at the dealership, I began making plans to open a used car lot of my own. I bought an ex-real estate building and had it moved to a leased location where I was going to start my business. My timetable to open my used car lot was six weeks away. I was about to give two-weeks notice and resign from my job. I really could not wait to be on my own. However, before my time was up, I was offered a chance to help check out a dealership that my current boss owned in Vancouver, British Columbia, Canada. I really could not pass up an opportunity like this! I still had my lot and my building and figured I could go back to that at anytime.

Two of us salesmen were sent up to Vancouver, BC for two weeks to see if we could help get the company out of a real bad spot the current manager had gotten them into. Vancouver was the same type city as Portland, only more beautiful. The people were very nice and we were very excited to be there.

After two weeks, we returned to Portland. The owners asked us how we liked Canada. We said that it was very nice and liked it very much. The owners asked John Kelly and me if we would like to go up there permanently, as managers. John would be the new car manager and I would be the used car manager. The general manager was Earl Richmond. He was a great public speaker. He had been with the FBI and head of security in Richland, Washington. He was a very good person.

We took a tremendous loss on our inventory. We had 800 new cars and trucks in stock, and the vehicles needed to be stored on a farm in the interim. Before we could enter Canada, we were told that if they were able to replace us with Canadian citizens, then we would have to leave. The replacements were required to have the same qualifications we had, and we certainly understood their reasoning.

I was able to enter Canada as a legal immigrant. While I was in Canada, I had a chance to meet some real nice people and was invited to their house. One in particular was Bill Colombus and his family—son Bill and daughters Darlene and Arleigh. They invited me to their house and we had hot apple juice and rum. We became very good friends. It is a nice feeling when you are in a foreign country and you can make a lot of friends. I met and visited a lot of people. Canadians like to party and have fun.

In the meantime, a miracle was happening back in Portland. Elaine was giving birth to our first child! We were so excited that our dream was coming true. We could have had the child born in Canada, but Elaine's doctor was in Portland and we had our home there. The child was the answer to our many prayers and desires.

My wife gave birth to our son Michael J. Pistoresi on January 8, 1952. Cigars were smoked everywhere and we had many great celebrations to honor his birth. We were honored with another miracle on September 16, 1953, when my wife gave birth to our beautiful daughter Danise Helene Pistoresi, and again we had more great celebrations and a lot more cigars were given out. Michael and Danise were very good babies. When we would take them to a restaurant, they never created a disturbance.

At St. Charles Church in Portland, Oregon, where Michael was baptized. Vernie (Curly) Monfils was godfather to Michael.

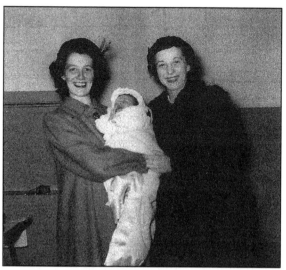

At Michael's Baptism:
Elaine and Mary Erceg Seats. Mary is Godmother to our son Michael.

Elaine and Mary at a party at Mary's house.

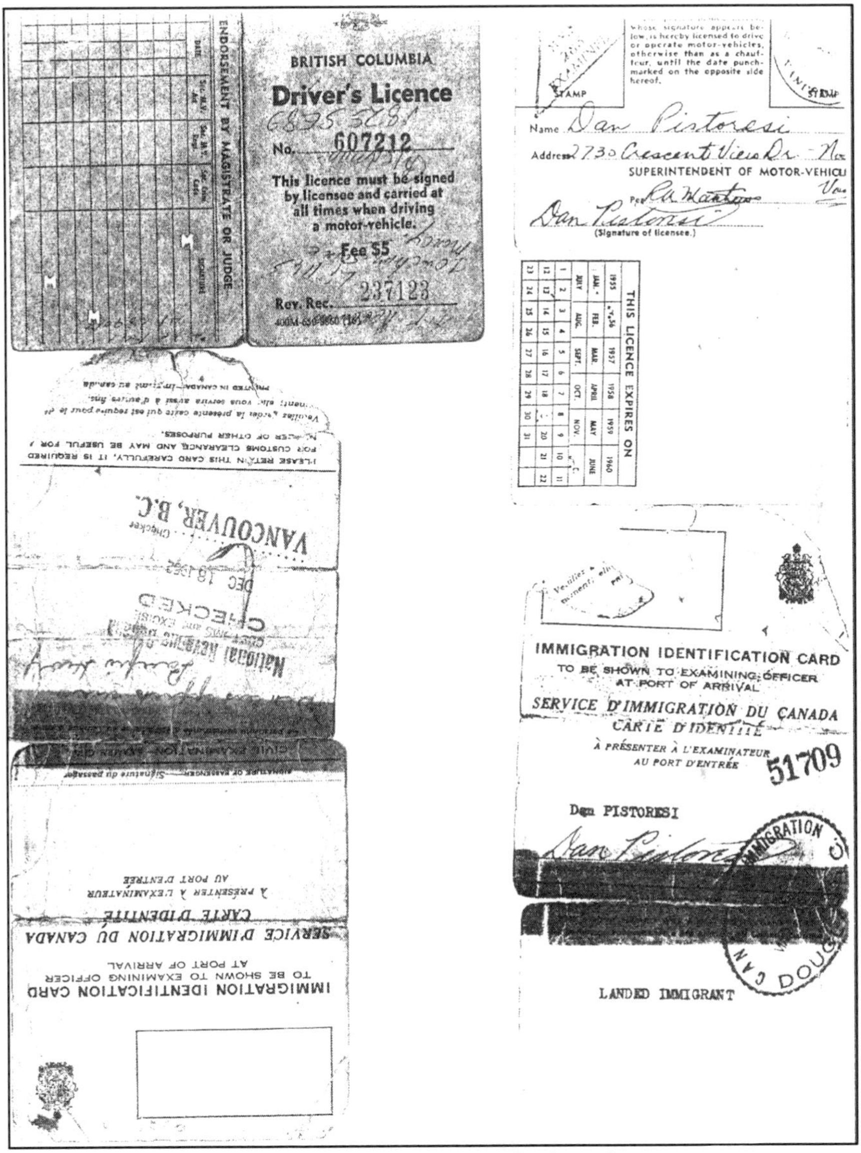

I was a landed immigrant in Canada.

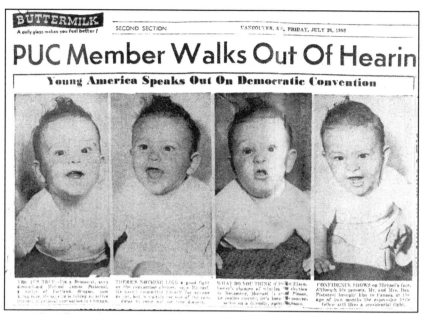

**Our first miracle son, Michael J. Pistoresi, born January 8, 1952.
Coming to Canada to speak his first words.**

While in Canada, I met Father Pete McGuire, a real rugged priest who was pastor at Saint Francis de Sales Catholic Church in Burnaby, just outside of Vancouver, BC. He had been quite a baseball player in his younger days and had received several offers to play professional baseball, all of which he had turned down to become a priest. I would visit with him and his brother and often had breakfast with them.

Elaine and I decided to make a complete move to Canada, so we rented out our house in Portland and turned around and rented a house in Vancouver, BC.

My wife was just as excited as I was to have the great pleasure of living in Vancouver. When we were settled in, we liked to go to the small Catholic churches because they seemed more friendly. Maybe they weren't, but this is how we felt.

One of our customers, a miner, mentioned that his very good friend was a priest at the Chinese Catholic Mission and he suggested I go to that church to meet him. Elaine and I went to his church and met Father Leonard and his brother Jack, who helped with the parish. After going to mass there a few times, we got better acquainted with Father Leonard and, during a conversation, he mentioned the need to raise money for the church. The parish was very poor. The nuns taught English to the Chinese-speaking people. Father Leonard said something about a bazaar and it sounded like a good idea. He had less than a hundred parishioners and it excited me to be asked to help in trying to raise money for the parish.

My wife and some of her friends made aprons, cookies, cakes, and napkins. The nuns helped in getting different items from vendors. Bing Crosby gave us a wallet (I was very disappointed that he did not give more).

One of my friends was the manager of his father's electrical wholesale outlet for small appliances. I went to see him and told him that I needed some appliances. I picked out thirty or so items and asked if he would deliver them. He said he would and then asked me for the money. I told him that he was going to be involved in a great cause and his donation would be appreciated. He said no, but he would give us 25 percent discount. I told him that was not enough to be recognized as a sponsor. After a long dickering fiasco, he ended up charging us only ten percent of the total bill and he did deliver the appliances.

We used to rent searchlights at our dealership and I called the owner and told him that I needed his help with furnish a searchlight for the bazaar. I told him we were putting on a fundraiser for the Chinese Catholic Mission. He told me no, and that he was not even Catholic. I told him that we did not care what he was, and would gladly accept his generosity. He laughed and said that he would give us the lights at half price. I told him that half price was not enough and he gave in and let us have the lights at no charge and he would operate them. This church needed all the money they could muster. The nuns were so devoted. They worked long hours getting ready for the bazaar.

A bookie friend of mine, Oscar Bodnar, worked for an oil company and liked to take bets on fights and horse races. I talked him into running the gambling at the Bazaar with card games and a roulette machine.

The church building was so packed with people that it was shaking. The searchlights really brought in a lot of people. This was a very successful event. We took in a few thousand dollars and provided a lot of fun for the patrons. Father Leonard could not believe how well it went over and was very happy.

Vancouver, British Columbia, has some of the best restaurants. Next door to our used car lot was the Vancouver Hotel, and across the street was Oscar's Steak House where they served the best Porter House steak and great clam chowder. Oscar took a liking to John Kelly and me.

One day when we were eating in his restaurant, Oscar came over to us and said he had a couple of friends that he wanted us to meet. We walked into the back room, and sitting there was Jimmy Stewart, Danny Kaye, Jan Pierce, and some of their managers. We were very happy to meet them. The Mills brothers would occasionally come in and we would sit and have coffee with them. When the top stars came to Canada, they played at the Palomar Night Club, right next door to Oscar's Steak House.

On another occasion, Oscar asked John and me if we liked to watch boxing matches and we said yes. He handed us two ringside tickets to see a championship fight. Cockell, from the British Isles, was going to fight Kid Mathews from the Seattle area. They were fighting open air at the Sicks Stadium in Seattle. This was a very good fight, but Kid Mathews lost. Oscar paid our expenses to go watch the fight.

Not long after, Oscar was on a mercy mission and the passenger plane he was on crashed and he was killed. That was the first time I attended a Jewish funeral. We missed Oscar very much. We had become very good buddies.

We had more than thirty salesmen working for us, and we became the largest Ford dealer in Canada.

On our used car lot, next to the Vancouver Hotel.
In car: Dan Pistoresi and Harry Davidner.
Standing: Jimmy Williams, who had been with the RCMP before he worked for us.

**Empire Motors, our used car lot on Burrard Street,
between Georgia and Robinson, next to the Vancouver Hotel
in Vancouver, British Columbia, Canada.**

I sponsored a car for the Jalopy Races on a quarter mile track. Our car won the 200-Lap Quarter-Mile race in Edmonton, Alberta. We came in second on the 300-Lap Quarter-Mile race. We had a white and blue car, and our tow truck was white and blue, and we towed it from Vancouver, B.C. British Columbia, to Edmonton, Alberta. They consider a driver when he belongs to the Turtleback Club. You had to have your car rolled over. All these drivers gave them 100 percent effort from the last place finish to the first place winner.

The Vancouver Hotel was next door to our used car lot and we would go there to eat. They served the best food at the most reasonable prices. Something exciting was always happening at the hotel. The British Empire Games were going to be held in

Vancouver and there was a lot of excited anticipation about it. Prince Philip was there for the games. His Austin limousine was parked on our lot. He was very much liked by the Canadians. The closest I got to the prince was six feet away.

The Canadians like the queen very much and have the deepest respect for her. The city of Vancouver was excited to have the royal family and the British Empire Games held in their city.

The Fire Department had an old fire truck with an outhouse connected to the rear that they planned to drive in the parade. Joe Doherty and a couple salesmen and I were admiring the unit. Joe got up in the driver's seat and noticed that the key was in the ignition. We all looked at each other and that is all it took. Joe started it up and we all hung on, driving down Granville Street going toward the airport. The siren was going full blast and we had a lot of people hooked on. When we got back, some firemen were waiting and they were very angry with us because we took the fire truck on a joy ride. We were very lucky that we did not get a ticket for what we did.

We were lucky to see all of the British Empire Games, a once in a lifetime event. During this great event, the lobby of the Vancouver Hotel was packed. There were so many people that there wasn't even six inches of empty space between both entrances, which are 200 feet apart. Both doors had at least 100 people attempting to get into the lobby. When they celebrate in Canada, they really celebrate.

When St. Patrick's Day rolls around, the Irish salesmen tell us they won't be in the next day. This is their big celebration.

One of our salesmen had a bad drinking problem and was getting many DUII's. He had a beautiful family and was a terrific salesman and a terrific person. I wanted to help. I told him if he would not take a drink for thirty days, I would fly him and his wife to San Francisco. They would stay at the Fairmont Hotel for three days and two nights with spending money included. I had a bottle of liquor, a box of chocolates, and flowers for his wife. I knew he would have a drink. He told me that he drank just a little bit. He did cut down on his drinking. The wife said to me that this was the first vacation where her husband had been sober in ten years. They told me they both had a good time and really, that is all that counts.

The Canadians celebrate Thanksgiving on a different date from the US. Al and Peral Moss invited our family, plus Flo and Jim Williams, and her sister and brother-in-law, and a few other friends for a great feast for all of us. We ate so much. The men watched TV and took naps on the floor, while the girls were in the kitchen washing dishes and getting the desserts ready. They woke us to let us know it was treat time. This was just like going to a banquet.

There is one holiday that we should copy from the British, and that is Boxing Day, held the day after Christmas. Before I ever knew of Boxing Day, I had always thought the day after Christmas should be a holiday. During the early days the royal families, the lords, and the wealthy, would give their servants and the poor their Christmas dinner leftovers the day after Christmas.

We enjoyed and loved Canada so much that we purchased a new house we figured we would be living in for a long time. If you have never been to Vancouver, BC, Canada, you are cheating yourself. It is better than any European tour. This is my sincere opinion. We made a lot of very true friends in Canada. If I were to have a choice of what country I would live in, other than the greatest country in the world—the United States of America, it would be Canada. Australia would be my third choice.

I had many chances to open up my own dealership or to run one. The company I was working for, Wayne Management, decided to move out of Canada. I hated to see that happen. I could have resigned and stayed in Canada, but I was with the company for a few years and they had been very good to me, so I decided to stay with them. They offered me a general manager's position in New York at Luxor Lincoln Mercury Dealership.

This was our last party with all our employees and friends.
I organized this going-away party on our departure from my second home in Vancouver, BC, Canada. I loved Canada.

The time had come to make arrangements to move out of Vancouver, BC, and Elaine and I put our house up for sale. It sold very fast. But then I turned down the offer to go to New York and decided I would rather be in a warmer climate. I decided to go to Long Beach, California, to work at Salta Pontiac, owned by the same company I worked for. Mike Salta was part owner, then he bought the others out and became the sole owner. Salta Pontiac was a very well run company. I was the used car manager and we did so much business that it kept us humping. I would get one day off a week and Elaine and I would take the kids to Knott's Berry Farm, Disneyland, and Marine World. This was all a very great treat. On every day off, we would plan something to do with the children.

My wife has an aunt that had worked for Raymond Novarro before he was murdered. Novarro was a silent movie star before talkies. After his death, the aunt went to work for Ethel Barrymore. Ms. Barrymore told Elaine's aunt to invite us to meet her.

We went over to her house in Pacific Palisades and Ms. Barrymore had me sit at the foot of her bed. My wife and I were so thrilled to meet her. We also met her son Sammy. Ms. Barrymore was bedridden at that time. She wanted us to come on a Wednesday so we could meet Frank Sinatra, Lauren Bacall, Humphrey Bogart, and some other stars that would drop by to see her often.

Elaine was pregnant for the third time, but ended up having a miscarriage, which was very disappointing. Mike Salta wanted my wife and me to be godparents to some of his children.

One day my wife cried and asked me if I had seen the newspaper article about three children who had been left on the church steps. I told my wife I had not yet had a chance to read the paper, but I asked her how the kids were doing. She replied, "How did you know?" I said, "I know you."

We decided to take the children into our home. The Los Angeles newspapers and the TV stations wanted to publicize this, but we told them that if any news gets out about this, we would not keep the children. We did not want anyone to know who we were. We asked them to just mention that the children are in good hands. We were only concerned about the children's safety and wellbeing. We knew we would have to give them back when the authorities found their parents.

SAFE HAVEN—Waiting wistfully at Juvenile Hall for parents who abandoned them Thursday night on the steps of St. Joseph's Church are Michelle Puz zola, 5, and brothers, Raymond, 3, and Michael, 4

Times pho

'God Fed Us,' Says One of 3

August 24, 1957. My wife Elaine picked up these children
and brought them to our house in Rolling Hills, California.

We really enjoyed having the children with us and they were
very nice. You have to wonder that deep down they must have
gone through some scary emotions. It makes you feel so bad to hear
and see these things happen. The media honored our wishes and
we did have the children for quite awhile before their parents were
located. When they found them hiding in San Diego, we were told
that we had to give up the children. We were asked if we would

97

mind taking them to San Diego to their parents. When we arrived at the parents' residence, we found that they had all kinds of games and TV that they were enjoying for their own selfish fun. We were really very disappointed in their actions and would have taken the children back with us in a heartbeat if we could have.

The drive back to Long Beach was very long and sad. We were so worried about the children but there was nothing we could do. The apartment they lived in was a wood structure, and in our opinion, it was a firetrap. There are very sad situations that happen and we have to do all we can to help the unfortunate and try to prevent these disasters. We have to take very good care of children and let them grow up without fear and abuse. All children need love and affection, guidance, and education to have a chance in life. It is our responsibility to see that they get this. To have a child and to give them your fullest love is the best feeling you can ever have.

Women should not get an abortion because there are so many couples that would love to adopt their babies. If you ever think that you might want an abortion, please talk it over and really think it out for a long time; go over all the pros and cons. The aborted child could have been a great scholar, a genius, or maybe grow up to be the president of our great country. I feel that the only times abortions are justified are in the cases of rape, incest, cruelty, or if the life of the mother is at stake. Otherwise, I do not believe in abortions and anyone that performs one commits evil.

When I was working at Salta Pontiac, we did a lot of advertising on TV. We sponsored Morey Amsterdam and I think Regis Philbin appeared on his TV show. This was around 1956. We also sponsored Spade Cooley, who was one of the hottest country-western singers in the USA. He was so popular that when he was on Bandstand live at our dealership, and pointed at a particular car and told the spectators it was a car he liked, that was all it took for people to come running to buy that car. Customers actually pushed each other out of the way for the chance to get to Spade Cooley's choice of cars. This would have been hard to believe if I did not see it with my own eyes. Periodically, I would do a survey to find out why the people came to our dealership. My survey showed that 25 percent of the people said that Spade had sent them in. He was a very big draw card.

I left a very well run and profitable dealership. But in leaving, I was able to remain with the same company. I went to San Diego to help run the dealership there, with a chance to buy in. The general manager was Marty Dubow, and he was the person I anticipated going into business with in a fifty-fifty partnership. I was very happy to get involved. I had a lot more assets than he did, but that did not matter.

Marty wrote up the contract for us, and when reading the document, I saw that it stated that down the road, if he wanted to edge me out, he could. This was like a bomb ready to explode without notice. This was not a good way to start a partnership. So I told Marty he could have my shares and I would bow out of the buyout and take my assets. I liked Marty, but going with his way for the partnership would not work for me and my family. When something starts to be different in a business transaction, the best thing to do is walk away and you will be farther ahead.

I loved San Diego. One of the managers, Tom Dotson, had been working at Tufford Motors before I arrived. We have been very good friends for more than 55 years. He and his lovely wife Joan live near Carson City, Nevada. He is a rugged outdoorsman and likes to hike, fish, and hunt. Tom and Joan are very nice people to have as friends.

While we were still in San Diego selling cars, we dealt with Admiral McGregor, the technical advisor for the movie *Run Silent,*

Run Deep, which starred Clark Gable. Admiral McGregor had a car leasing company and was thinking of buying some cars from us. He was a very nice person to talk with, and to listen to because of his stories. San Diego was really a strong Navy town and a very nice place to work. It was also a very nice place to live because of the weather and their very nice restaurants.

My wife and I believe that things happen for a reason and we should not question those reasons. Sometimes we wonder why certain things happen. I did talk to my wife about breaking away from going into business with Marty Dubow because it would have been a short-term adventure. You have to believe that God really watches over all of us. I do not like to make major decisions on the spot. I like to think them out. I feel that if you wait, you have a better chance of having a clear head when it comes time to make a major decision.

The night before I made my final decision with Marty, I received a call from Harvey Benson, a salesman I worked with when selling cars. He was in the San Diego area and wanted to get together with me. He told me that he and Fred Reed, a very good friend of mine, were going to open an American Motors dealership in Redwood City, California. He wanted to know if I would join them. He told me that I would have 25 percent ownership, and 25 percent of all the dealerships that they might acquire in the future. I could not refuse this great opportunity. They had much more money than I had. They were wealthy. Things went really nice, and we bought out the San Carlos Point dealership that was only a couple of miles away. This was good business.

While I was in Redwood City, a salesman I had hired and trained in Long Beach, California, wanted a salesman's job with me. I hired him and it turned out he had a friend he wanted me to hire also. Which I did. The salesman I trained was Ray Sutton and his friend's name was Hank Soma. They were both above-average salesmen.

My partners and I started getting things together and began adjusting to life in Redwood City, which, according to the government, is considered to have the best weather in the USA. We were doing very well. Later, my partners were offered a Rambler dealership in Richmond, California. They had me look at it, and I determined it might be a good point. They asked me if I wanted to run it, and I said I would like to. And I did get my 25 percent as promised. Ray Sutton wanted to come with me, and I was happy to have him.

So far, my partners had lived up to their promises. And when another American Motors dealership became available in the Santa Clara, California, area, my partners bought it. This time, however, I did not get my 25 percent ownership. They did not keep their promise, which hurt me because I had so much trust in them. I still liked them as friends, but not as business partners.

We really had a nice dealership in Richmond, California. My friends and partners lived in Woodside. Fred lived across the way from Frank Buck, who had some of his animals there. Fred and his wife, Alta, wanted us to buy their house at a very low price—it was worth a lot more than that. But Woodside would have been too far a commute for me from Richmond. Their house was very beautiful. It had a swimming pool and was on an acre of land. That was really hard to turn down.

I won a contest to fly to Mexico with my wife, and meet up with other dealers from all over the Northwest who were the winners in their districts. This was a very nice vacation on American Motors. We went to Acapulco, which was a dream place and a lot of fun. From there, we headed to Taxco, where they had silver mines and made very beautiful silver jewelry.

The Mexican people were so very nice to be around, and we visited with many of them. The bullfights and the Jai-Alai games were exciting to watch, and their restaurants are second to none. The only thing wrong with a vacation is that it ends too soon, especially when you are having fun. The bullfights may be brutal, but they have been going on for hundreds of years and the meat is given to the poor. If you have doubts about bullfights, you should go to the slaughterhouse and see out how your filet mignon, New York steak, porterhouse steak, and other meats that end up at your table are produced. I went to a slaughterhouse for my first and last time and saw how the cows were slaughtered. I consider that the bullfights are very tame in comparison to the slaughterhouse.

A Smooth Way to Get A Partner Out

My partners did complete their buy for the Santa Clara dealership. That location was one of the best places you could ever dream of getting. But I did not get my 25-percent interest. They sold their soul cheap. When we first got involved, my partners told me that they did not want to make much more money. They said they would give me their shares in the Richmond agency if I would give them my shares of the Redwood City agency, which was a more profitable dealership.

Richmond had a lower income-earnings per household by at least 40 percent, compared to the Redwood City area. I was not in a position to challenge their request. It is always easier to get rid of a minor partner—but it really is a bad way. I will not do business this way because it is immoral.

The name of our company was Friendly Rambler and we changed it to Melody Rambler. I promoted Bill Wilson as the new car manager, and Ray Sutton as my used car manager. I gave them each the great opportunity to buy a 12.5-percent interest in my company. They did not have to sign any capital loans; that I was able to do on my own. And they were not responsible for any contingent liability. I also offered that anytime I acquired other dealerships, they would have the same opportunity to acquire a 12.5-percent interest of said company. All my agreements were done with a handshake, and I honored every one of them. Your word should always be your bond.

I was a 25% owner of this dealership in Redwood City, California, 1958.

While our new company was in operation, we sold a lot of cars. With one particular customer, we had to do a lot of dickering over the price of the car, but finally the sale was made. When we were writing up the contract, we advised him to purchase credit life insurance to pay off the car in case of his death or in case he lost his job because of an accident. We explained that his payments would be made with no worry to the family. Some people like that kind of insurance and some do not like it. I like it because at times it is a necessary evil. We all worked very hard to convince the customer to purchase the insurance. With everyone's help, I sold him on buying the policy. I was very happy he did agree. After we completed our sale, he told me he liked football games and that the Oakland Raiders was his favorite team. I always received a lot of tickets for different sport events because I was so involved in sports. So I gave him three tickets to the Raider's game the next day, with seats on the 49-yard line. He was so tickled, he could not believe what was happening.

The next day, which was game day, just before noon I received a call from his wife that he had just died. He never had the chance to see the game, and this was really a shock to all of us. This was so hard to believe. Since this happened, I was so happy that the car he bought was going to be free and clear with no worry about payments. The customer's wife told us that she would not have been able to make the payments on the car.

One week went by after this tragedy and the office manager told me that a person from Republic Insurance Company, which insured our credit life policies, wanted to talk to me in private. I went out to meet the person and during our conversation on the showroom floor, he mentioned that since it was a Friday night that they purchased the credit life insurance, his company could get away without paying the claim.

I heard this beast, but I told him to explain it again because I did not understand what he said. After he repeated his statement, I asked him if he could see our showroom window and if he was not out of my sight in fifteen seconds I was going to throw him through it (you scum bag). I would say that he knew I was serious and he could not get out fast enough.

I called the insurance commissioner and explained what took place and told him what I said to the insurance agent, and he said, "Good for you."

A young man, Jim Ruddell, came to our dealership trying to sell us some advertising. He was a cocky nineteen years old and I could tell he was a good prospect as a salesman for our company. I let him make his pitch and after he finished, I asked him for his paperwork. After he gave me his paperwork, I tore it up and told him not to waste his time trying to sell junk advertising. I offered him a chance to sell a good product. He joined our staff and he turned out to be a smart kid and a very good salesman.

We were in the process of hiring a finance and insurance manager, one of the best jobs in a car dealership. I told the sales force that the first person to get his insurance certificate would get the position. This was the only fair way to do it. Everyone had the same chance to get the position. The job was awarded to Jim Ruddell because he was the first one to get his certificate. He had a sharp mind and was good at everything he took on. Within six months of learning to play golf, he was shooting in the low 80s for eighteen holes. He told me how good he was playing tennis, so I took him on. I could tell after his first two serves that he was a better player than I was. But I played my best tennis match that day. I could not miss even one return serve. I beat him 7 to 5. He wanted to play more, but I told him that I did not have the time. He knew he was a better player than I was. If this had gone on longer, he would have won the last five sets. I was lucky to beat him once.

When you are in business, you should do all you can to help promote goodwill and participate in community activities. This is a good way to have your business in the news and lets the citizens know you care, especially when it involves children.

I wanted to do something different at our dealership, so we had a circus come to the showroom in Richmond, California. We had a carousel for the kids, plus real lions and monkeys, and elephants the children could ride. We gave out free hot dogs and popcorn, and everyone had a very good time. And, we did sell a lot of cars.

I also held a coloring contest for different age groups. The judges were art teachers and the winner of each age group received a savings bond. All the runner-ups got a trophy. This made the children happy, having everybody a winner.

This is our dealership in Richmond, California, where I put on a circus.
Next to the elephant is Ray Sutton, a salesman I hired in Long Beach, but he
wanted to work for me in Redwood City, then here in Richmond.

We held a coloring contest for children—all of them were winners.

Our office staff served as hostesses for our circus.

One day we had a couple of black Americans trying to sell me advertising for a black-run newspaper. These were two very sharp young men and the more I talked to them, the more I was impressed with them. We became very good friends. They talked me into joining the NAACP, and I gave them $500 for a lifetime membership.

I asked Clifton Jeffers to consider selling cars, and he decided to take me up on my offer. I also told him he was really too smart to sell cars and that he should be a doctor or a lawyer. I said it takes a lot longer and is harder to become a doctor than a lawyer and would require much less work. I said being a lawyer would be easy for him.

Clifton Jeffers' wife taught political science at San Mateo Junior College. Just before I hired Clifton, one of the salesmen came to me and said if I hired this black American salesman, the others were all going to quit. He let me know he was speaking for the other salesman. I said, then Clifton and I would be the only ones working the next day. At the sales meeting, all the salesmen were present. I introduced Clifton to them and said, "I don't know why Clifton wants to sell cars with us dummies. He is much smarter than us."

My dear friend Clifton Jeffers in our Richmond, California showroom. Jeffers was the first black American salesman hired in Northern California. He is an attorney now.

After Clifton was with us for a while, I asked him to tell me how I should refer to him—as a Negro, an American, a colored American, or a black American. He said black American. We liked each other, so we could talk to each other like that without either of us taking offense. This is the way we can all learn. I told Clifton he was prejudiced, and right away, he said he was not. I told him that he did not want to live around Haight-Ashbury. He said, "That's right." I told him all of us – no matter our color, race, or creed—want to better our way of life. He agreed. Clifton decided to enroll at Hastings Law School, which is a topnotch law school in the country. We helped him some and felt real bad that we could not attend the graduation ceremony after receiving his invitation. The last I heard, Clifton is still practicing law in San Francisco, California.

I was invited to a few black caucus meetings when the Black Panthers were making a lot of noise. At one meeting, I said riots were not the way to get things going to benefit blacks. I said that through economics, they could get further ahead. I suggested they buy where blacks are hired and the others will get the message. I told them it was a tough row to hoe, but they would get their say and their way in time. This was in the late 1950s, early 1960s.

I met Jackie Cooper who was the head of the March of Dimes at that time. He was a very nice person to talk to and very friendly. All of us liked him very much. The March of Dimes paid all of our expenses. I didn't like that because we were supposed to raise money, not spend it. I feel that anyone who has the honor to be chosen to head a charitable organization should be paid a small salary, just enough to cover room, meals, and normal expenses. When we would raise money for the boys' clubs, it would all go directly to them. I won the contest for selling the most day-old newspapers. We were very proud to be able to help.

We were involved with the March of Dimes.

HIGH-KICKING PONIES—Here is the Melody Rambler nine that finished first in the Richmond-San Pablo-El Cerrito Pony League race. In the back row, left to right, are coach Wes Greenwood, sponsor Dan Pistoresi and manager Caesar Perales, Sr. Up front is Carlos Perales, the club's bat boy. Players are, front row, left to right: Bob Preston, Noel Price, Donovan Nutt, Dennis James, —Independent photo by Bob Forsburg Steve Meahan and Caesar Perales, Jr.; and, second row, from left: Gary Chaires, Mike Warwick, Wendell Horton, Larry Carrigan, David Perales, Philip Robbins and Leonard James. Absent from the picture were coach Larry Sheppard and players Russ Martin and Calvin Kelly.

Back row center: Dan Pistoresi, Sponsor.

When we opened our dealership in Richmond, I wanted to talk to the best attorney. When I met Fred Bold, I gave him a $500 retainer fee. I told him that I would probably never need him, but I wanted him as my attorney. I did use him twice for our two adopted sons.

Our agency sponsored a lot of ball teams and I was director of four boys' clubs: San Pablo, El Sobrante, El Cerrito, and Richmond. We were also involved with the March of Dimes for Contra Costa County and attended a meeting in Los Angeles.

Our showroom in Richmond, California.
The highest sign is 60 feet tall.

When President Kennedy was in office, he encouraged everyone to keep healthy and to exercise. During this time, some of my friends in Vancouver, British Columbia, Canada, came up with a Hooter Scooter that was a one-seater. This unit had four wheels, a ratchet cord, and you steer it with your feet. We had a few prototype models built in Japan. The people who got this project started were Gordie Bergman, Huddy Hall, Mr. Solomon, and I. We had more than a thousand units sold before we started production.

Mr. Solomon was very close to Kroger's main office in Cincinnati, Ohio, and he set up a meeting with them to distribute our scooter. They liked the idea and wanted to know how much we were expecting out of each unit. We told them we wanted one dollar from each unit. They offered us 25 cents each. We were very smart, and stupid, for not accepting their offer. They had the best outlet to get our scooter out on the market. We also found out we could have them built in Texas for two dollars less per unit than the cost of building them in Japan. We should have gone along with Kroger's offer, which would have given us all a nice profit without doing anything. It would have also given us a chance to work on another project.

We took a bus to the Crey Cup Game so we could drink.
The bus took us to the gate and picked us up right after the game.
No chance for a DUII. And a lot of fun.

Hugh Moore, George Krachuck, me, and Gordie Bergman, in Canada at the Crey Cup. We always had a lot of fun horsing around.

Movie star Richard Carlson talking to three of our office girls.

We invited Richard Carlson, the movie star who, at that time, was in *The F.B.I.* movie series, to visit our dealership. I met Joey Brown at a friend's sporting goods store. He autographed a lot of baseballs so that I could give them out to the kids. When I was young, I used to see Joey Brown in a lot of movies and I really enjoyed them.

In north Richmond there was a park that had a clubhouse and a cement basketball court outside. A great African American by the name of Charlie Reid was in charge of the park and took no nonsense. Charlie would have been in the class of your top professional baseball stars and he did help some of them. With his discipline for strict rules, he helped a lot of kids stay out of jail. I would have never known about his help to them except some of them confided in me. Charlie Reid held twilight basketball games, and a coach or two would show up, checking out the talent to see who they might want playing for their schools. As time went by, a lot more coaches came to observe the up and coming ball players.

I received a trophy for sponsoring events at Shields Park in north Richmond.

I had the honor of accepting a trophy given to me by this park for sponsoring some of their teams and furnishing their equipment. One day, I went to an auction of sports equipment and I bid on some of the equipment. After the third sale, I told everyone I was bidding on the equipment to give it to children who needed it real bad. They held back on their bids and let me get the equipment at a decent price. This made a lot of kids happy.

Outside of the Police Athletic League, which has been doing a wonderful job in efforts to cut down on crime, not much else is going on to address gang wars. Whatever has been done is not enough. Gang wars are getting out of control and I think I have a solution that might bring some of these disputes to an end. I would try to get the gang leaders together and talk to them one-on-one to find out what their real problems are. They would have to be assured that they would not be arrested, just put on probation for about three years. If he or she keeps a clean record, their rap sheet will be cleared. Most gang leaders can manage their members and get them to do whatever they want them to do. Which is why I think this method could work. We could never stop all crime, but perhaps we could cut down on some of it. A life of crime often starts out due to home life and when the kid drops out of school they remain unemployed and shunned by their peers. They probably feel as if no one cares about them. Let's give them a lifeline. Not all will take it, but some will.

I feel as though a large percentage of these poor souls really do not like what they are doing but they got sucked in and didn't know how to get out. Perhaps they became comfortable as a member of a gang.

We have more and more people committing crimes, but they're still walking the streets because they've never been caught. They've managed to stay out of jail.

We waste money trying to stop crime because we don't try to find jobs for these kids. I suggest we try to get them back in school and teach them a trade. Some of these girls and boys have great minds and could become great citizens if we gave them some attention. I would exclude molesters, rapists and violent criminals from this program because they are usually inclined to repeat the offense.

When I was in the car business in the San Francisco Bay area, a probation officer called me and asked if I would consider hiring a person who had recently been let out of prison. I told the office that I would, as long as the guy was not a molester, rapist, or had been convicted of a violent crime. I did hire the person and never mentioned the man's history to my employees or my family. The slip of a tongue can cause more damage. I ended up hiring ex-cons three times and never had a problem with them. I figured that giving the guy a chance at a new life was important. After working for me for a while, each of them returned to the towns they had come from.

SNIP—and there goes the ribbon and the new Melody Rambler agency in San Bruno is open for business. Left to right, we have Thomas Moore, United California Bank; Ed Sherrard, United California Bank, Burlingame office; Bill Wilson, Melody co-owner; Dan Pistoresi, Melody co-owner; Sandy Akers, Her Highness, Miss San Bruno; Ar- Irene Upshaw, office manager; Charlie Carman, sales manager; Mayor Dan Risso; L. F. "Stan" Stanley, president, Chamber of Commerce, C. L. Modesiti, district manager, American Motors, and John Romano, secretary, Chamber of Commerce.

Ribbon cutting at the San Bruno dealership I put together.

I was looking for another dealership and found a spot in San Bruno, California. It was a used car lot with a service garage, which I needed. Before I talked to the owners, I checked with the banker to see how much of a cap loan I could get. After driving him by the lot he said, "I will give you fifty thousand. With a closer look, I will give you more." I called the owners and asked if they wanted to lease their lot and building. They said no. I said would you consider $2,500 per month. They said yes. The going rate then was around $800 to $1,000 per month. I had already been approved by American Motors for a dealership.

When I got together with the owners, I leased the property for $1,100 per month. This was a very good piece of property, and I offered them a sales job. I gave Bill Wilson the opportunity to have a 12.5-percent ownership, and offered Ray Sutton the same percentage. This was all verbal. I told them what I would do with any expansions in the car business. Ray Sutton was in Sacramento, checking out a Chrysler Plymouth dealership and said he was thinking of going into the used car business. I decided I would let Bill Wilson buy Sutton's share. This way Bill Wilson could have a 25-percent ownership in the San Bruno dealership. It was a great opportunity for Bill Wilson to be the general manager and a vested partner.

The person who sold us the Richmond dealership had a salesman who had been with him a long time, and I could not figure out why the owner had not given him a chance to buy it. His name was Bill Wilson and he was a very good salesman.

Bill Wilson and Dan Pistoresi.
I put him into business as a minor partner.

Without Prejudice—My Personal Advice To Reverend Al Sharpton and Reverend Jesse Jackson

I was a lifetime member of the NAACP. I joined through Clifton Jeffers and Marty Dinkins. When we were in business in Richmond, one night some African-American boys roughed up my son. My dear friend Lonnie Washington, a policeman who managed our baseball team, heard what happened to my son and he wanted to go after the boys who had done the roughing up. I told him not to do anything. Make no police report. Report nothing to the newspaper. The reason I wanted this incident forgotten is that a confrontation like this can cause a riot and more hate. Our son was not hurt that bad, and I felt very good about how this was handled.

I hope that both of you—Reverend Al Sharpton and Reverend Jesse Jackson—take some of my advice because there are certain situations that need your leadership and I suggest you try to reason out a solution that doesn't cause unnecessary riots. I am not against peaceful marches because some are needed and they do help solve some of the problems. But not all.

Let us look back many years ago when Reverend Martin Luther King, Jr.—God bless his soul—broke through to help black people get some of the rights they should have had all along. It really took too many years for his dreams to happen, but now we are starting to get on the right track. There has been improvement, but still not enough. It will be better. Think about it a little. If you grow up in an environment where all you hear is hate for "others"— within your family, from other families, your schools, your city, state, and country—it becomes a brainwash, a powerful tool and a very ugly one. This is one of the main reasons hate festers. Children growing up in this type of environment learn that this is the only way to feel because they do not know better. But today, many have seen the light and are less prejudiced. They understand we are all born equal, no matter the color of our skin.

I was lucky my parents never had hate for anyone for they were my best mentors. I am so proud of them. My wife and I taught our children to respect everyone, no matter their skin color or religious beliefs. In order to solve problems, they first have to be solved at home. In time, I believe that 80 percent of these problems will be solved. We will never solve all of them.

Reverends Al Sharpton and Jesse Jackson, I know you mean well. I hope I am wrong, but to me, you two show hatred and create more hatred in the way you approach problems. You seem to think some of them are not even there. You are both intelligent pastors who can solve a lot of problems and stop some of these riots that destroy innocent people's property, including small business owners whose property has been destroyed. Remember, violence does not solve your problems. I think deep down you both mean well, but I think you are going about it wrong. I am 90 years old now and I have heard and seen it all.

God bless both of you and I wish you many good days ahead. Things will get better each day and all we have to do is strive for it on a positive path. Your guidance can help some of these situations, and I strongly hope you will take this advice.

The Excitement And Challenge Of Moving

I never did want to stay in one area or one house all my life because I wanted to know what was going around me. We moved a lot because of my jobs in the car business. It really is exciting to move to new places because you meet so many great people and establish a lot of new great friends.

I never drove to work or came home the same route. We all can easily become creatures of habit, but I did not want to get to be that way.

My advice is, go a couple of blocks out of your way at different times. This way you can see what is happening around you. You might find out that one of your friends might live only two blocks away, or maybe there is a house for sale you might like to own. At least, it will change your routine.

You might want to work in another country and learn their culture. If you go, you'll have a very good chance to meet some real nice decent people. I would not know some of my greatest friends from Canada, had I not moved there.

On our Vacation to Portland, Oregon.

One evening when we went into Jake's, we did not see our favorite waiter and were led to believe that he was not working that night. We were seated, and our orders were taken, but a couple of minutes later, here comes our favorite waiter. And he was so hurt I thought he was going to cry. He asked us if we did not like him anymore. I felt so bad because he was the one we wanted. When we left, I gave him five dollars. He did not want to take it. I made him take it. We asked him for his schedule so that we would not miss him the next time we came in. A waitress or waiter can spoil their customers' appetites. I've made it a practice that if I liked the way I was served, I return to sit in that person's section.

When you are a waitress or a waiter, you have an obligation to the people who hired you to do your best in serving your customers. You are a salesperson, and the way you treat your customers will encourage your customers to come back to see you again. You will help the owner stay in business, keep your position, and make yourself a very good living. Always work smart.

The Truth Comes Out

The time I lost the sales contest for the trip to Detroit and the tour through the Ford Factory I was able to go as the runner-up. I never did complain. Ten years later, when I went into partnership with my friends in the used car business, they asked me to join them as a partner in an American Motors dealership in Redwood City, California. That is when the truth came out. One of my partners told me that Mike Salta and Bud Meadows had him buy some cars so that Bob Action could beat me and win the trip. He said he had no choice because if he did not do it, they would not wholesale him any more cars. He told me that it bothered him so much that he had to tell me how I had been cheated. I knew I had really won and I was happy he told me how it went down.

I purchased the Chevrolet dealership in Rodeo, California, a few miles from Richmond. I was going to move it to Pinole. I had the property all set to build a dealership on. The Chevrolet dealership that had been in Richmond for many years complained to General Motors because they thought we would be too close to them. We lost out. The owners of the Chevrolet dealership were nice people and that is the reason I did not want to make a big issue of this. A very good friend of mine, Lonnie Washington, was active in the sports world and knew just everybody in it. He was also on the police force in Richmond. One day, he came in my office and asked if I would sponsor a semi pro baseball team. He said he had a chance to get new uniforms a major league team had turned down because there was a flaw in the cloth that you could hardly detect. I told Lonnie I would like to buy three full uniforms and suggested he get the other car dealers to buy the rest of the uniforms so all of us dealers could represent the city of Richmond. I thought that if all the dealers went in on this, it would be very good for the city of Richmond. Lonnie did go to all of the other dealers, and only one dealer agreed to sponsor just one uniform. When he came back to say how he made out, he asked if I would sponsor the whole team. I told him without hesitation I would be happy to be the sponsor.

Our team could hold their own with any minor league or farm team. They had a fundraiser for the March of Dimes and our team played against top major league baseball players including Willie Mays, one of the greatest people you could ever meet. He was so down to earth and just a regular guy. Vada Pinson, Broglio, Landis, and other greats rounded out the pro team. It was a great honor and treat to be able to see these great ball players that gave their time to help the March of Dimes.

I had a semi pro basketball team whose roster listed names like Cornell Green, who played for the Dallas Cowboys Football Team and was an All-American basketball player for Utah. Our team played in a couple of preliminary games for the San Francisco Warriors. We won the March of Dimes Tournament in Sacramento, California. I was suited up and they let me play a couple of minutes. I had a chance at two shots and missed both of them. After our team won, I took all the players out for a steak feed, with my son Michael, who was our team mascot.

I called the restaurant and made reservations for fourteen people. When we went in, the owner looked shocked because there were black Americans in the group. I told the players that we would have a drink before we ate, and another one after dinner. We all drank, ate our dinners, and everything went perfect.

Mays to Play in 'Dimes' Game Here

—Independent photo by Bob Forsburg

MAYS' MACE—Giant outfilder Willie Mays fondles a bat at a March of Dimes benefit baseball game meeting in Richmond. From left are Lonnie Washington, manager of Melody Rambler; Jerry (Skeeter) Matteri, Mays, and Winters Calvin. Matteri and Calvin are organizers of the game which will send Washington's team against a collection of big leaguers, including Mays, at Nicholl Park Sunday, Jan. 27, at 1:30 p.m.

Willy Mays played against our semi-pro baseball team. A terrific person.

In 1959, a salesman who had worked for me in Vancouver, B.C., came down to Richmond with his rugby team. They were going to play against the University of California, Drake, and other college teams. The Canadians were between 27 and 35 years old, playing against college kids. The teams' name was the Maralomas and they won the championship. They played in Monterey. They all signed the game ball and gave it to me. I still have it. I furnished them with cars so they could get around town. They stayed at a motel in Oakland, and when I went to see them there, I asked the motel owner how he liked them. He said that they were very nice, but to please tell them not to throw the lawn furniture into the swimming pool. It seems they liked to party and have a lot of fun.

Heads 'Dimes' Cast Tomorrow

Landis, Broglio On All-Star Bill

Major league baseball's best two centerfielders will be in the same lineup tomorrow for the annual March of Dimes game at Nicholl Park.

Willie Mays of the Giants, considered the best fielding centerfielder in the National League, and Jim Landis of the White Sox, rated tops with a glove in the American League, will perform for the Major League All-Stars.

Landis is expected to play center field to do it, 1 p.m. charity game with Mays moving to first base, according to Lonnie Washington, whose Melody Rambler nine is contributing players to the opposing Minor League All-Stars.

Game co-chairmen Calvin and Skeeter Mattei also have obtained the services of former Yankee catcher and current Rochester manager Darrell Johnson, Cardinal pitcher Ernie Broglio, Mel infielder Pumpsie Green, Indian pitcher Frank Smith, Met catcher Jesse Gonder, Redleg outfielder-third baseman Tommy Harper, Oriole-owned outfielder John Scruggs, and Indian-owned infielder Billy Williams.

Joining the Ramblers, semi-pro and former professionals making up the Minor League All-Stars.

Among the others will be Emery Phillips, Joe Dorsey, Willie Calvin, Ray Hamrick, Jim Reynolds, Jim Johnson, Mike Tatro, Bud McGee and Walt Pocekay.

There is no admission charge for the game. However, March of Dimes committee workers will be stationed outside Seawright Field to accept donations.

Broglio Sparkles

Third-place St. Louis closed to within four games of the Dodgers last night when Ernie Broglio checked the Reds on one hit in the nightcap of the Chicago doubleheader...

Ernie Broglio 10-7, struck out seven in his relief stint. Bill White and Charley James homered for the Cardinals, whose three-run fifth tagged Joe Nuxhall, 8-5, with the defeat.

Successive homers by Lee Maye and Eddie Mathews of former Calvin...in the third inning got the Pirates away from the Braves...and a three-run shot by...

DIMES GAME-MINDED—Although the above picture was taken three weeks ago at a Galileo Club banquet, these men had their minds on tomorrow's annual March of Dimes game at Nicholl Park. Seated, left to right, are New York Met Pumpsie Green and Chicago White Sox star Jim Landis, who'll play in the game, along with former Philadelphia Phillie and ex-Oakland Oak Ray Hamrick, second from left in the rear. Standing at the extreme left is Skeeter Mattei, co-chairman of the benefit game. Second from right is Charlie Reid, veteran molder of local baseball stars and at the far right is Lonnie Washington, manager of the Melody Rambler team which will take part in the Nicholl Park contest.

Richmond Cagers Top Burgies 77-58; Davis, Green Spark Winners

By GARY BROWN

The Melody Ramblers of Richmond, at times resembling the famous Harlem Globetrotters with their slick ball handling and shooting artistry, thumped the Sacramento Burgies 77-58 Sunday night at Sacramento High School to capture the sixth annual March of Dimes Basketball Tournament.

A highly-receptive gathering of 1100 watched. All proceeds from the tournament went to the March of Dimes. The event was sponsored by the city parks and recreation department and The Union.

The Burgie five, dotted with Sacramento State College players, matched the Ramblers shot for shot in the first half until the Richmond quint poured on the coal in the last few minutes before intermission to stake out by 36-25 at halftime. The winners led comfortably throughout the second half.

DAVIS LEADS ATTACK

Fred Davis, a remarkable little guard who managed to shake loose under the bucket repeatedly for tips and follows, led the winners with 19 points. Cornell Green, who played for Utah State this year, had 15 for a big assist.

Gus Lovett hit 16 to pace Burgies, most of his shots from underneath and at short jump shot range. Bill Whitaker hit 10.

The Burgies had a well-oiled attack but they were beat to the punch often on the boards, both offensively and defensively. Then, too, the Ramblers were able to work the ball in for easy buckets while Burgies had to fire often from long range and then hit only sporadically.

The Burgies and Ramblers stormed up and down the court like a wild yo-yo during much of the first 10 minutes of the game.

SHORT-LIVED LEAD

Burgies led by scores of 3-0, 5-4, 7-4, 9-8 and 11-9 before relinquishing the edge for keeps at 13:41 when Phil Hart, another pesky guard with an artful jump shot, rimmed one from six feet out to haul the Ramblers out in front 12-11.

Lovett's free toss tied it at 12-12 but Cornell Lacy stuck one in from 15 feet out and Hart stole the ball and drove the length of the floor for a layin to make it 16-12.

The two teams traded basket for basket in the next six minutes although the Burgies could rally no closer than two or four points most of the time.

With 4:30 left in the first half, the Burgies were very much in contention at 26-22, but then Joe Dorsey hit two free throws, Hart hit another from underneath, Lacy registered two more on a steal, Green hit two gift throws and Hart connected on a hook as the Ramblers moved out by 36-22. They led at halftime, 36-25.

COULDN'T CLOSE GAP

The Burgies played the Ramblers on even terms through the early moments of the second half and at one point colsed the margin to eight points at 49-41 with 13:05 left. But after the Burgies closed to nine at 51-42, the amazingly quick Richmond ball hawkers splurged for seven points and moved out by 58-42. That broke any resistance the Burgies might have offered in the final 10 minutes.

The Ramblers stayed in front by at least 10 and as many as 15 the rest of the way.

UAW 550	F	G	T	ALBURT'S	F	G	T
Rapp	8	7	23	Lane, L.	8	3	19
Searfoss	1	1	3	Washington	4	1	9
DeVight	0	0	0	Davis, W.	7	3	17
Brown	1	1	3	Davis, R.	6	5	17
Perez	2	0	4	Gardere	8	9	25
Gonzales	1	1	3	Lane, M.	0	0	0
Hart	2	0	4	Guess	2	0	4
White	1	1	3				
Dixon	0	0	0				
Brady	0	0	0				
Totals	16	11	43	Totals	35	21	93

Melody Ramblers	G	F	T	BURGIES	G	F	T
Lacy, C. ..	3	0	6	Munson ..	2	1	5
Green	5	5	15	Baker	0	4	4
Hart	5	2	12	Rohrer	3	2	8
Hardeman	1	0	2	Whitaker	4	2	10
Davis ...	7	5	19	Skov	0	2	2
Causey ...	2	0	4	Lovett	7	2	2
Perkins ..	1	2	4	Rankin	1	0	2
Dorsey ...	3	2	8	Dille	3	1	7
Fields ...	0	0	0	Pugliese ..	2	0	4
Gordon ...	1	0	2	Nelson	0	0	0
McKinney	2	1	5	Barker	0	0	0
				Mitchell ..	0	0	0
Totals	30	17	77	Totals	22	14	58

Halftime Score: Ramblers, 36.25.

Our team wins against Sacramento Burgies.

JAMES L. MERRIHEW
SUPERINTENDENT OF SCHOOLS

DAVID C. GRAY
PRINCIPAL

RICHMOND UNION HIGH SCHOOL
1250 TWENTY-THIRD STREET
RICHMOND, CALIFORNIA
94804
June 7, 1965

Dan:

A short note from us thanking you for sponsoring our winter league
baseball team this year and in the past. We have really appreciated your
generosity. You have helped some of us go on into higher baseball such as
college and professional baseball as well as giving us the opportunity to
play and enjoy playing. You certainly have helped us enrich our lives.
Once again thank you.

Jim Kirk

Tom Champion

Mike Serrano

Patrick Joyce

Albert Harrison

Lee Ballard

Wayne Lovejoy

Albert Harrison

Lonnie Page

Gary Whittemore

Mike Cooper

C Gampa (Kansas City M')

Dick Foster

Gary Wheatley

Leroy Dickens (Minnesota Twins)

Jerry Luzar (Univ. of Calif)

Emery C. Phillips (Coach R.U.H.S.)

COLT CHAMPIONS — Celebrating their Richmond-San Pablo-El Cerrito Colt League championship are (front row, from left) Bob Preston, Tim Kennedy, Gary Chaires, batboy Clarence McIntosh, Bob Sale, Mike Merriman and Caesar Perales Jr. and (back row, from left) manager Caesar Perales Sr., Leonard James, Willie Adger, Ken Corcoran, Steve Meehan, Howard Hatton, Howard Rew and coach Warren Grant.

—Independent photo by Prentice Brooks

BEST BY TEST — Only recently a tourney winner in Sacramento, here is the Melody Rambler basketball team that added to its laurels last night with an 81-70 win over Newell's Meats for the Martinez Invitational Tournament title. Standing, left to right, are Jerry Jackson, Tom Cousey, Phil (Bo) Hart, Cornell Green, Joe Dorsey, George Fields, Clyde Hardeman and Freddie Davis. Kneeling behind mascot Michael Pistoresi, son of Melody Rambler general manager, are, left to right: John Perkins, Cornell Lacy, Carl Gordon, Pistoresi and Charles (Cha-Cha) McKinney.

We won the Contra Costa Independent League Tournament.
My son Michael was mascot. I played a couple of minutes.

Our team won the March of Dimes Tournament in Sacramento, California.
Mascots were my son Michael and his friend.

I did get the great pleasure of meeting George Romney and
had the opportunity to converse with him for a short time. There
was a long line behind me and those people also wanted to have the
chance to talk to him. He was a very gracious man. This happened
in Oakland, California, where we had the American Motors
showing.

Novato, California, was an exclusive area that every dealer
wanted to have a franchise in. While still in Richmond,
representatives from Toyota and Datsun (which is Nissan now)
tried to entice me to take on their cars. I liked Toyota the best, but
thought that Nissan was a strong second. Toyota Corporation
invited more than thirty car dealers from Northern California to try

and talk them into taking on their franchise. Mr. Toyoda and Jim McGraw, their general manager, tried to sell us on the franchise and were not getting very far. I got up out of my chair and walked to the podium and asked if I could speak to my fellow dealers. I told all the dealers that Toyota was like a junior Volkswagen, a very hot and popular car. A Toyota franchise is what we all need. Ninety-five percent of the dealers signed up and they elected me president of the Advertising Association. I was re-elected for three straight years. I got Bill Wilson, my minor partner, into a Toyota franchise and talked others to join up as well. Many dealers laughed it off and I know they are not laughing now.

The Toyota people were very smart. The car they had been manufacturing before I was involved was not a very good car. They dumped it and started to make a real good car. Their first pickup was a very good truck, but it did not have much room for the driver. The vehicle was built for smaller people. They changed this right away. Toyota now has very good cars and trucks.

We took a white Toyota and put 12-inch wide racing stripes on the hood, top, and trunk, and had a potential customer drive it in first gear, as hard as he could, then the same in all gears. We ended up putting 19,000 miles on it and it really stood up. All those miles were put on with rough driving by everyone.

During the time, I had the American Motors franchise, George Romney was head of the American Motors Corporation. He was the one who made Rambler one of the best cars ever made, next to Mercedes Benz. When we received our shipment of cars from the transport trucks, the time it took to get them serviced and ready for sale was a lot less time than it took for Ford, Chevrolet, and Chrysler vehicles. The AMC cars were built better. The worst thing that happened to AMC was when George Romney left. I had the pleasure of meeting him and had my picture taken with him. Every dealer was very unhappy when Romney left.

Mr. Abernathy became the president of AMC, and compared to George Romney, I would rate him much lower. Abernathy was a nice person, but not a great leader. I attended a car show in Las Vegas and when Mr. Abernathy made his speech to all of us dealers, he said we would be number one and drown Ford and Chevrolet. We were a solid number three, way ahead of Chrysler.

I was disturbed by his remarks. Ford and Chevrolet were in the major league and AMC was the best in the minor league, and getting better all the time. We were a threat to Ford and Chevrolet, which is why they started to build a compact car as a challenge to the mighty little American. This alone indicated that American Motors was a great threat. Not one of the other company's small cars could compare to the Rambler. But they were able to steer potential AMC customers away, especially those loyal to Ford and General Motors.

I purchased the Chrysler Plymouth dealership in Richmond and used Northwest Management Company. We had a very good reputation in the car business. We rarely lost a salesman, but if they thought that the pasture was greener on the other side and left, then changed their mind, we would hire them back only once. I treated everyone in the same manner I would expect to be treated.

My wife and I won a trip to Jamaica and Haiti. This was a wonderful trip. The only bad part of the trip to the islands was to see the poverty that existed in this area. The Jamaican people were so nice and very friendly. We did enjoy Jamaica very much.

From Jamaica, we headed to Haiti, which was poverty-stricken and worse than Jamaica. We went sightseeing, and when we got to the palace, I tried to take pictures outside the gate. One of the guards had a rifle pointed at me. We were really scared and did not get any photographs. They really had great brandy, which came in many different flavors. They also had great glass works. We bought a few items and one of them was a glass ashtray that weighed a ton. We went back to our cruise ship and we were given the choice of heading for New Orleans or for New York. I love New York, but nothing will compare to New Orleans.

Our friends, the Bidulphs, wanted to go to New Orleans with us. We had so much fun. When you are away from home, it is best to have another couple with you, for safety reasons.

There were oyster stands on the streets of New Orleans and my wife had never eaten an oyster. It turned out she loved them and ate a dozen oysters. I ate a dozen myself, but I really love oysters.

We made the rounds to the best eating establishments, and wherever you eat in New Orleans, you will get the best food. Al Hirt was playing and we got to see him and a lot of other top entertainers. We purchased one of Al Hirt's records, which he signed. New Orleans is a fun city to visit.

The vacation was perfect until we arrived home to witness a person walking in front of our dealership carrying a sign that said we were unfair to our employees.

The union had never talked to me about wanting to organize our staff. Our mechanics were union and we paid them higher than union wages. We had one mechanic who wanted more money because he could do twice the work of any other mechanic and because he never had any repairs come back for further fixing. Because he belonged to the union, I told him I would call the union hall and see what I could do.

I called the next day and talked to the head of the union and he told me I could do nothing. This kills the incentive to try to get ahead. We had two different unions picketing the dealership. I really had to think fast because a lot of people will not cross a picket line and it ends up costing a lot of money. I am not against unions because they do a lot of good, until some of them got into racketeering practices.

So, I went to a modeling agency in San Francisco to interview some models. I had them come to our house and let my family decide which one to use for walking alongside the picketers. She would be carrying a sign saying we were caught between two unions trying to organize our salesmen.

The sign said, "What can we do? Help!"

The model we chose was very beautiful and she sure got attention.

GOOD ANSWER—When Melody Rambler auto agency in Richmond was hit by picketing in a union jurisdiction dispute, owner Dan Pistoresi countered with a picket of his own, pretty Susan Black, 22.

The model we hired with our sign.

Melody Rambler was picketed while we were out of the country.

I had to call the National Labor Relations Board to set up a meeting with them. The meeting was held and I told them what I was going through and that the strike was costing us a lot of money. I told them to do something to protect me. They were starting to be negative with me, and more or less said they could not do anything for me. I jumped out of my chair, raised my voice, and said they had helped the Southern Pacific Railroad! They came back at me saying the railroad was a very large company. I shot back that as an individual, I was as big or bigger than the railroad.

My words seemed to amaze them and they caught on to what I was trying to tell them. They set up an election. The salesmen voted and the two unions never got one vote. We won, but we lost because the unions would not accept defeat. I was told by some union friends that our dealership was being blackballed by the unions trying to organize us. What really hurt was the fact that we had the best working conditions for auto salesmen in the Northwest. Much better than the union could even think of offering.

Every Christmas, we would have a party for the kids. I had a list of every employee's children with their names, birthdates, and gender. I would go to a toy distributor and buy each one an appropriate gift. I would write down what I got them each year, and the next year they would get a different gift alternating dolls, games, skates, stuffed animals, cameras, and bikes for all ages. Some of the kids grew up, got married, and if they had a family, we would add their newborn. We did this for twelve years. This was my wife's great enjoyment.

We also gave out Christmas bonuses and each family would get a large laundry basket full of food for the holidays. We did the same for Easter and Thanksgiving. I really do miss doing this. We provided the best medical plan we could buy, plus we furnished a $10,000 life insurance policy payable to their family. We would take the fathers and their kids on chartered boat fishing adventures.

Our service manager had a fatal heart attack at work when he was in his early thirties. The insurance and the state covered only a portion of his salary, and we made up the difference. This was the right thing to do and it pleased me to be able to do this.

A very good salesman that worked for me in Canada wanted to work for us, and I was very happy to hire him. He was with us for about six months then became seriously ill. He passed away a month later. The $10,000 life insurance policy really helped his family. His wife bought a gift shop in one of the hotels in San Diego, California, and became self-supporting.

On one of our fishing trips we hosted for shop and sales people took place in the San Francisco Bay, just past the Golden Gate Bridge.

When you have employees, you do have to help them understand that sometimes the benefits you get from your employer can make the difference in your life. Most of the salesmen we hired had never sold a car or truck before, and some never had any sales experience of any kind. This really gave us a chance to train them the way that we wanted them to sell, with no previous hang-ups. If any salesman quit, I would make sure that their insurance remained in force for a month after leaving.

One day, when I was coming home from work, a lot of children were playing on the lawn having fun. Our Dalmatian, Prince, was playing with the kids. I noticed one boy, who lived a couple of blocks away, who had never played at our house before. He was older than the rest of the kids. A short time later, when I was in the house, I heard a scream and found the boy had been bitten in his calf, and the bite drew blood. The boy was on top of Prince, trying to ride him. I was worried about the bite and went right over to his parent's house to see what I could do for the boy. We took care of all the expenses. I found out later, from other kids, that the boy was a bully who had snapped tails off cats. I still felt sorry for the boy.

We had to quarantine Prince, and the vet who took care of him told us that Prince would not bite anyone unless the person was trying to hurt him. I thought everything was taken care of. We were forced to give Prince up and we gave him to a friend of ours. We'd had Prince from when he was six months old to eight years old. Our children were angry and did not want me to give him up. We had gotten Prince from a friend while living in Long Beach, California, and the kids had fallen in love with him. When we originally brought him home, the first night, when the children were sleeping, we went in to check on them and Prince was at the foot of the bed. As we entered, he growled at us because he was protecting the kids.

Three hundred fifty days after the biting incident, we read in the headlines of the newspaper that we were being sued because of Prince for many thousands of dollars. I told the insurance company not to pay. We would go to court. They would not listen and paid them off. Then the insurance company cancelled our policy.

The boy's father sold supplies to doctors and hospitals. Some of our doctor friends were angry for what the father did and told my wife and me that they were going to quit buying insurance from him. I was happy about their concern, but I told them that the father still had to make a living. Before the settlement was made, the boy who had been bit would limp around, and immediately after the settlement, he was seen running. Isn't it funny how after an insurance settlement is made, people heal up real fast.

All the time that I spent in the car business, I learned a lot about people, and car dealership owners that gave me the time to make my own observation and see what the playing field was like. Some of the things that I observed I was determined not do, and some of the things I decided I would do if I were ever the owner of my own place.

My suggestion is, if the place that you were working was profitable, when you decide to open your own place, take 75 percent of how they operated and allow the remaining 25 percent to be based on your own personality and ideas. This will give you a greater chance of making it in business.

I learned real quick that married salesmen with families who are working entirely on commission had nervous wives because they never know if their husbands were going to earn enough to pay the house expenses. When I hired a salesman, I wanted to get the worst fears of the wife out of the way.

During this time, the average wage was $500 to $600 per month. I would guarantee the person $600 to $1,000 per month. For example, if the guarantee was $600, on the 10th of each month, we would give the salesman $300, and on the 25th of the month, he would receive the other $300. Then, at the end of the month, if his commissions amounted to $800, pay him $200 to settle for the month. If he made only $400, he was never charged back. When the new month started, he started fresh. The wives told us that paying their husbands this way gave them no worry about money problems, and it took the monkey off the salesman's back.

I.N.J.

St. Patrick's School
Rodeo, California
September 12, 1961

Dear Mr. and Mrs. Pistoresi,

Greetings in our Lady! Thank you for the many, many ways you helped us so that we could enjoy our trip from Tucson. We certainly feel indebted to you for your untiring generosity. May God reward you and your beloved family by an abundance of both temporal and spiritual favors. A Novena of Masses is being offered in the Shrine of the Little Flower in San Antonio, Texas for your intentions.

Again, many thanks to you and rest assured of our community's daily prayers for you as our benefactors.

Asking God's blessing upon your loved ones and your family, I remain

Gratefully yours in Christ,

Sister Mary Dolorosa, C.M.F.
Sister Mary Dolorosa, C.M.F.

DAN PISTORESI OFFERS PRAISE FOR RAMBLER STAFF

Dan Pistoresi, operator of the Melody Rambler agency in Richmond, declares he has never forgotten that "I was once an automobile salesman." This explains why he has been instrumental in setting up higher working conditions and compensation for auto salesmen in the northwest.

The Melody Rambler agency is credited with being among the top in working conditions in the United States. Benefits include hospitalization and opportunities for employes to invest in the company.

An added activity is the sponsoring of teams in all kinds of sports, including semi-pro baseball, winter and summer league softball, high school teams, winter league bowling, little league teams and pony league teams.

Pistoresi's staff includes such well known people in the auto distribution field as:

Bill Wilson—Has interest in Melody Rambler, Richmond, and Melody Rambler, San Bruno. Started as a salesman with the firm and rose to sales manager and, because of his loyalties and capabilities, was given an opportunity to purchase stock. After the firm acquired the San Bruno Rambler agency he was promoted to general manager and vice president with the option of purchasing more stock.

Les Telburg—Parts manager and service manager. Previously he spent 10 years as a representative for General Motors.

Sam Cortese—Service manager, San Bruno. Previously with American Motors for 15 years. He joined the Melody Rambler firm six years ago and worked his way up to general sales manager.

Dale Rosenberry—Started as a salesman six years ago and worked his way up to sales manager. Now working for Melody Rambler at San Bruno.

Glen Whalen—Accountant, has been doing business for Melody Rambler for the past six years. He became closely interested in the firm and finally purchased shares in Casa de Chrysler-Plymouth. He holds a vice presidency.

Barbara Kerr—Joined the organization more than five years ago as an office girl and worked up to the position of business manager of Melody Rambler. She trains other girls in the office and recently became a member of Quota Club.

Dan Pistoresi—Maintains controlling interest in all companies while permitting key personnel to purchase shares. He declares, "Behind every man there is a woman, and in my case it is my wife, Elaine, who is my inspiration. She also serves as secretary for all my companies.

"In the Melody Rambler organization a person's age does not have any bearing on promotions. It's ability and attitude that counts."

Ed Holmes—Comptroller of all the companies; general manager and treasurer of Casa de Chrysler-Plymouth. He joined the organization after many years in all phases of the automobile business because of the opportunities available with Dan Pistoresi.

Roy Ellison—Started as salesman, became an insurance department manager. He has done an outstanding job of helping customers solve their financial problems in the purchase of automobiles.

Flo Terrel—Became a member of promotions in the organization after many applicants had been interviewed. Flo was chosen because of her knowledge of business management and her congenial personality.

Duane Derksen—Started with Melody Rambler four years ago as a salesman and is nod general sales manager at San Bruno and doing an outstanding job of assisting Ed Holmes.

George Allen—Has been with Melody Rambler for four years. He started as a salesman and is now general sales manager working directly under Dan Pistoresi.

Lane Harper — Started with Melody Rambler four years ago at the age of 21 and became the youngest parts manager in the country. He became the service manager two years ago and is a past president of the Northern California Parts & Service Managers' Association.

145

We furnished our salesmen, managers, and office managers with a new demonstrator for their personal use. Doing business this way made it easy to attract a strong caliber of person. Ninety percent of our staff was promoted from within. When you hire real good people, you should know them well enough to train them for managerial positions. We must have trained them fairly well, because other dealers were always trying to hire them out from under us. I was very strict that no one who worked for us, at any of our places, was allowed to use foul language, especially around our office ladies.

The day I heard an irate customer swearing at our office girls, I went out and told the customer that these girls were not used to hearing this type of vulgar talk. He apologized to the girls and went out and bought them each a box of candy. I shook hands with all of my employees every day.

Ray Sutton, my partner, took an interest in a blonde girl who bought a station wagon from him. This customer owned a small restaurant and, to me, it seemed like she had a lot of money from operating such as small restaurant. With my gut feeling, I told Ray to be very careful. I told him she looked like trouble.

Shortly afterwards, the car buyer was in an accident back east. The police discovered plates to make counterfeit ten and twenty dollar bills. It turns out that the woman and her partner had been printing money in the back room of the restaurant. A lot of policemen ate there and the woman did attract a lot of men. If not for the accident, they probably would never have been caught. I think that the plate artist was killed in the accident. The police, later on, told us that the counterfeit plates were so close to perfect that an expert would have had a hard time determining if they were real. I told Ray Sutton to watch his step a little closer. He did learn a good lesson, for the time being.

One day when I was looking at the newspaper, I noticed an article about an Italian village, Villa Montelone Rocca Doria, in Sardinia, that the government would do nothing for. I cabled the mayor of the village and told him I was very interested in their story and offered the buy the town. The Italian government did not want the townspeople to sell their village, and told them that if they agreed not sell the village, the Italian government would build an aqueduct to augment the village's meager water supply. They made this gesture only after they found out that the villagers decided to sell their town.

I could not believe how much publicity this generated. I received more than twenty deals offering to sell me things like a monastery, a hotel, and a villa. I think a lot of Italy's con artists took an interest in me. I figured that buying a village could have been a great investment at that time and if I could not do it myself, I had friends who indicated they would like to get involved.

> ? ? ? ?
> Dan Pistoresi, the imaginative Richmond auto dealer who bid to buy that Sardinian village, is still awaiting word on his offer. But he's received all kinds of other communications from around the world. One offers property for sale in Genoa and another says there's a good buy in Rome. So far though Dan is only interested in Monteleone Rocca Doria. Word is expected in about a week through an Italian bank on the price and so forth.
> ? ? ? ?

The INDEPENDENT Mon., Oct. 23, 1961—3

WANT TO BUY A TOWN?
HERE'S ONE IN SARDINA

SASSARI, Sardinia (AP)—Want to buy a town?

All 300 residents of Monteleone Rocca Doria have put theirs up for sale or fair trade, with lavish enticements about its "ancient churches, fantastic view and exceptional climate."

The townfolk met, talked it over, decided unanimously, and put this advertisement in Sardinian newspapers:

"The longtime residents of Monteleone Rocca Doria, disposed to move elsewhere, will sell or trade on reasonable terms the entire community, 30 miles from Sassari and 20 miles from Alghero, located on the summit of famous Roccaforte, 1,110 feet above sea level.

"The town has ancient churches, a city hall, orphanage and new schoolhouse, a fantastic view and exceptional climate. For information, apply to the town residents."

What will happen to them?

They are willing to move anywhere else. Anywhere, they agreed, would be better than trying any longer to eke out a living in Monteleone Rocca Doria.

For there are no jobs there. The town is off the beaten track, with no main roads passing near.

1961. This town was up for sale or trade.
I wired the Mayor about it.

148

(Turn to Page 2, Col. 6)

Richmonder Bids To Purchase Poverty - Stricken Italian Village

By BUD WAKELAND
Independent Staff Writer

Richmond auto dealer Dan Pistoresi says it's no joke that he's interested in buying a scenic but poverty-ridden village in Sardinia.

Pistoresi, whose parents were born in Italy, read in The Independent Monday that the town of Monteleone Rocca Doria had been placed on the auction block by its citizens.

He immediately fired off a cablegram to the mayor asking the price, if a trade might be arranged and how much land and how many buildings are involved.

"I simply felt that it might be a good real estate investment," Pistoresi said today. "The land is apparently barren but I figured that its scenic beauty might make it valuable as a resort."

The Associated Press reported today that the 300 villagers may not have to sell after all.

DAN PISTORESI

The Sardinian regional government has promised them a road to link the isolated mountaintop town to a nearby highway. They were also promised bus service to nearby towns and an emergency water supply until an aqueduct can be built.

And they were assured that the regional council would reconsider a project to create an artificial lake which villagers had complained would flood the only flat, fertile piece of farmland nearby.

The village elders have agreed to think it all over but so far they've refused to withdraw their offer--and Pistoresi is still interested.

Operator of Melody Rambler, Inc., the genial, 37-year-old Pistoresi says he'll buy the whole works if possible or even part of the town. So far no cash offers have been received by the mayor.

"Even if I can't make the deal," Pistoresi added, "I'm happy that

He Wants To Buy Village

(Continued From Page 1)

my offer has apparently done a lot of good for the village. That's wonderful."

The auto dealer, who lives at 2500 Arlington Blvd., El Cerrito, said he is completely flabbergasted by all the interest in the transaction.

He had planned to take a trip to Italy next year anyway with his wife and three children and win, lose or draw, he's now certain to take in the advertised "fantastic view, ancient churches and exceptional climate" of Monteleone Rocca Doria.

After the Mayor received my message.

149

Ex-Portland Man Offers To Buy Italian Village

An ex-Portlander, now a Richmond, Calif., businessman, has offered to buy a bankrupt and poverty-stricken Italian village in Sardinia.

Dan Pistoresi, owner of two automobile agencies in Richmond, made the offer when the village fathers of Monteleone Rocca Doria, a remote mountaintop community, put their town on the auction block.

Pestoresi, whose parents, Mr. and Mrs. Guy Pestoresi, 3434 SE 17th Ave., were born in Italy, cabled the mayor of the village, offering to buy Monteleone Rocca Doria. He has not yet received a reply.

"The village is still considering my offer," Pistoresi told The Oregonian. "As far as I know mine is the only one they have received."

Aid Offered

Pistoresi, a former restaurateur who left Portland about eight years ago, said the Italian government has asked the village not to sell out. The government, Pistoresi said, has offered to build a highway to Monteleone Rocca Doria to encourage tourist traffic to the picturesque village. The government also promised to build an aqueduct to augment the meager water supply.

These offers came, Pistoresi said, only after the 300 villagers decided to sell.

"I simply felt that it might be a good real estate investment," he said. "If my information is correct, the village could be developed into an excellent mountain resort. If my offer accomplishes nothing else, it will at least have forced the government to pay some attention to these poor people."

Pistoresi said he was not told what price the villagers want for their combined properties. "If the amount is too much for me to handle alone," he said, "I'm sure I could raise additional funds."

TOWN TO[

An Italian immigrant talked proudly of his son's success in the automobile business, but admitted he has no idea why his son Dan has offered to buy an entire Italian village.

The proud father is Guy Pistoresi, 3434 SE 17th Ave.

His son Dan is an automobile dealer in Richmond, Calif.

A month ago when Dan (A Benson High School graduate) learned that the poverty-striken town of Monteleone Rocca on the Italian island of Sardinia had been offered for sale, he fired off a request to the mayor.

According to the senior Pistoresi, Dan hasn't received a reply yet.

The 300 residents of the isolated Italian town were upset over poor bus service, poor roads, and inadequate water supply. They wanted out.

Dan Pistoresi is interested in buying all or a part of it. He has requested the detail n cost, terms, trade possi ility, and how many building' re involved: He feels i' might be a good real estate nvestment."

Dan has never seen the Italian village. Neither has his father, who was born near Florence, and came to this country before the first World War.

Buying an Italian Village.

The last report I received was that the villagers were still hoping the Italian government would live up to their promise. At least, due to the publicity, the Italian government did take notice. The squeaky wheel does get all the grease. It pays to be heard.

I sponsored the Ms. Bronze Contest. I also gave out scholarships to help young people because I feel it is the duty of every business owner to address this. We all must help when we can, no matter who is in our great country. I sat as a judge on the Junior Achievement Awards in Berkeley, California. I was president of the auto dealers in Richmond, California, and I was the director of four boys clubs in Contra Costa County. I contributed for the film to be made for the visually handicapped in the East Bay area. This was through the Berkeley Unified School District in California.

For our New Year's party in Santa Rosa, I had a bus take us there because I did not want anyone driving after drinking and we stayed overnight at the El Rancho Inn so no one suffered with a hangover. This was a good way for our salesmen and staff to play it safe and enjoy themselves.

Our company furnished St. Albert's College with some cars, and they also purchased a few cars from us. We would advise them as to when it was a good time to trade them back in for new models.

I called the Catholic Church Diocese in San Francisco and told them I would not sell them any cars, period, but I would let them know when it was a good time for them to purchase their cars, and how to do it. I really had nothing to gain except I knew I could save them a lot of money. I felt good knowing I could help the Diocese, but felt bad when they said they did not want my help.

We tried to get a new bank started, which was to be called the East Bay Bank. The State Banking Commissioner in San Francisco would have authorized capitalization of $2,100,000. Some of the large banks used some strong language to stop us from getting our bank going. We had a great lineup to be credible in having a new bank started. All of us directors were in different related fields that would make our bank very strong, and that did put a worry on some of the other banks. Our president had been a banker for many years and an expert on the ins and outs of banking.

I suggested to Bank of America that they should hire some black Americans. Bank of America was visited by Colonel Leon Washington, the publisher of *The Sentinel.* He brought along TWA hostess Ms. Brea A. Berry, to show her that the bank did not have any black employees. This was in the Inglewood area and in south central Los Angeles.

It took a long time before Bank of America came to their senses and hired a black American to work for them in Richmond, California. Black Americans made up almost 50 percent of the people living there, so this was a real disgrace to all banks in the area. I want to say that pressure without violence can get things accomplished in due time. Sometimes due time takes a little too long.

In 1963, the Salesian High School held a campaign to raise $100,000 to build a football field, a track, and two baseball diamonds on the property they owned. I was selected for the committee assembled to help raise money.

11-30-1963

New Bank Planned at San Pablo

A new bank, which would called the East Bay Bank, is planned for the city of San Pablo, it was disclosed today when an application was made with the state banking commissioner in San Francisco.

The bank would have an authorized capitalization of $2,100,000.

If approved, John F. Varni, of 2812 Shane Dr., Richmond, former Bank of Pinole manager, would become manager. He would also be on the nine-member board of directors, each member of which would own 1,700 shares of stock, valued at $51,000.

Other directors would be Oran W. Davis and Leland F. Reaves, the attorney for the group, both of Richmond; Alfred M. Dias of San Pablo; Jack D. Kilcrease and Harold V. Taylor, both of El Sobrante; Dan Pistoresi and Herbert H. Reeves, both of El Cerrito, and Simon Siegel of Orinda.

Seventy-five sponsors will be entitled to hold up to 400 shares each. Reserved for employes will be 1,200 shares.

And the public will be allowed to purchase 23,500 shares; no shareholder would be allowed more than 200 shares.

BLACKLESS BANK—Col. Leon Washington, Sentinel publisher, points toward the door of the Bank of America branch at 5930 W. Century Blvd. to show TWA hostess Miss Brenda Berry that the branch has no black employes. The bank services parts of South Central Los Angeles and Inglewood.

Auto's New (Lucky) Owner

—Independent photo

CARDOZA'S CAR, NOW — Tim Kennedy, left, student body president at Salesian High School, and Bill Belan, right, chairman of a win-a-car contest at Salesian, watch as Doug Cardoza prepares to drive off in the car he won. The auto was donated by Melody-Rambler, represented by Dan Pistoresi.

"A LADY'S DREAM," MISS FALCON CONTEST NOW ON

by Vickie Norman

This year the Miss Falcon contest will be a spectacular and will be presented in pageant, music and drama. Young ladies between the ages of 16 and 24 have been invited to participate and the selection committee chose Elaine Christy, Shirley Davis, Theresa Dixon, Ruth Garrett, Gloria Head, Deborah Hughes, Margie Goudeau, Jackie Johnson and Annette Rhone as the first group.

Officially ready to begin, some of the first entrants caught the eye of the photographer as they shared their happiness over being selected with some of their friends over the telephone in the reception room of the Falcon Publishing Co. on Market Street in Oakland. Jon Fifer, "Mr. B. Nyce," served soft drinks and coffee to the group in this relaxed atmosphere. As one can see these young ladies are an attractive, brighteyed group. The Selection Committee finds them surprisingly intelligent and talented.

The queen this year will be selected by judges and three-point perspective basis: Scholastic Attainment, Talent and Beauty. The presentation will be followed by a Grand Parade in downtown Oakland with unusual floats representing bay are business enterprises and social, civic and fraternal organizations.

Lovely Deborah Hughes of Richmond was the first sponsored contestant our good friend and yours, Dan Pistoresi of Melody Rambler of Richmond. This man in the auto dealer business, has done more public work, financially, than any other individual in the San Francisco Bay Area. He draws no color line we it comnes to advertising, sponsoring athletic teams—a man with a heart really. The young lady whom he chose to sponsor is a June graduate of the University of California, Berkeley campus, and she lives with her parents. Other contestants and their sponsors will be listed in this column as they are officially released by the Selection Committee of the contest. Velma Ford (Mrs. Ralph Bradley) is in charge of the contest this year and she, Mrs. Gay-nols, va oning from ri kle Norman.

DAN PISTORESI SPONSORS UC COED IN FALCON CONTEST

by Vickie Norman

Attractive Deborah Hughes of Richmond, a June graduate of the University of California, Berkeley Campus, is being sponsored by one of California's most distinguished gentlemen, Dan Pistoresi of Melody Rambler, Inc., with offices in Richmond, Albany and San Bruno in the "Miss Falcon 1962" Pageant.

This year's contest, "Lady's Dream," will be a musical drama, and will be presented in the Oakland Auditorium Theatre, Sunday, Sept. 30, 8:00 p.m. The pageant will follow a parade by contestants and last year's winner, from Berkeley to Oakland and led by Travis Air Force Base Honor Flight Drill Team and Color Guard.

Dan Pistoresi is a modest philanthropist and loves children of all ages, races and creeds. He has numerous pet projects—a semi-pro baseball team, a basketball team and has contests on coloring for ages 4 to 14 to encourage would-be Van Gohs. He gives freely of his time, his money and especially generous to athletes in all sports. In fact he is keenly interested in almost anything beneficial to mankind—in this case the presentation of Negro beauty at its best. He chose both beauty and brains in sponsoring Deborah Hughes. She received her Bachelor of Arts Degree in mathematics from the University of California in June and will enter the Berkeley campus this fall. She will work towards her Masters. Her ultimate goal is her Doctorate. This congenial Miss is (in her own words) "Especially grateful to Mr. Pistoresi" who is sponsoring her in the pageant, "and to the wonderful people who awarded me the Spencer Scholarship (A 4-year scholarship covering tuition, books, transporation, etc), my sorority, Zeta Phi Beta, who gave me financial aid during my undergraduate days ot UC."

As one can see, this year's pageant is timely, beautywise and wise in the ways of physical fitness, what with a sports enthusiast as a sponsor and Dan Pistoresi is one. As one can see, also, Miss Hughes is photogenic, a mathemetician, as a contestant, a philanthropist for a sponsor, A lady's Dream will become a reality for some lucky miss come September 30.

Falcon Contest Sponsorship.

—Independent photo

DRIVE—Among those leading a $100,000 fund ations campaign to finance a new Salesian High cthletic field are, from the left, Father Arthur Peiti, administrator at the school; Assemblyman n Knox, co-chairman of a committee; Dan Pistoresi, committeeman; John Toffoli, committeeman; and Joseph Genser, co-chairman. The field would be located on 10 acres now owned by the Salesians. It will consist of a football field, a track and two baseball diamonds.

I was on the committee to establish a football field, a track, and a baseball diamond, 1963.

My wife, Elaine, was involved with the Live Oak branch of the Children's Hospital of the East Bay. She would help on everything that would help children. She is a terrific mother. That is why I am so proud of her. Elaine was always ready to help on any projects that involved young children. She would drop any appointment that she might have just to be of service for children.

VISITING Eddie Bryan, five, of Richmond are Mrs. Daniel Pistoresi, left and Mrs. Edward O'Halloran of Live Oak Branch, Children's Hospital of the East Bay. Branch members will volunteer aid when East Bay-Polack Bros. Circus comes to Oakland Auditorium Arena, July 10-12.

My wife Elaine was always ready to help.
This was at Children's Hospital, East Bay, California.

BECAUSE of the large number of tickets sold for Live Oak's "Day at the Races," additional luncheon tables were set up in the beautifully redecorated lounge at the Turf Club where the races and results were projected on television. Mrs. Bruno J. Roveda, right, greets Mr. and Mrs. Daniel Pistoresi, left, and Mrs. Kaho Daily, seated.

—Independent photo

4-24-65

A fundraiser for the Children's Hospital, April 1965.
From left: Elaine and Dan Pistoresi, Mrs. Kaho Daily, Mrs. Bruno J. Roveda.

18—Saturday, May 4, 1963   The INDEPENDENT

Live Oak Preview Luncheon

LIVE OAK BRANCH Children's Hospital of the East Bay, previewed two taped future broadcasts of the Ernie Ford television show after a luncheon at Orestes last week. Participants included Mrs. Dan Pistoresi, left, Live Oak member, with guests Mrs. Kenneth Hood, center, and Mrs. John Cute, in the car. Checking the road map are, from left, Mrs. Larkin Smith, Mrs. Walter Moore, Jr., Mrs. Carl Watson, Mrs. Clifford Moore and Mrs. Walter Moore Sr.

—Independent photos

My wife Elaine on another fundraising project for the Children's Hospital.

One day I went into a barbershop to sell some of these day old newspapers. The barber was cutting someone's hair. I asked him for a donation for the Boy's Club and he said he was busy. I told him that I was also busy, trying to get money for the Boy's Club. I did get ten dollars from him, and the fellow who was getting his haircut gave me five dollars. I gave the tickets to the barber and he said, "Why didn't you tell me that you were selling tickets?" I said, "If I did, you would buy two and think you were doing a big thing."

ORIENTAL gardens were arranged at Mira Vista Country Club for the annual fall dance of Acorn Branch of Children's Hospital of the East Bay. Those attending "Oriental Splendor" included Mr. and Mrs. Dan Pistoresi, above left, and Mr. and Mrs. Jim Arata; and, In photo at right, Mr. and Mrs. John R. Walker and Mr. and Mrs. Don Dewey. Proceeds benefit the part-pay program at Children's Hospital.

Setting up a bowling fundraiser for the Boys Club.

When it came to raising money for the Boy's Club, if I had to embarrass or shame anyone for that good cause, I would do it. If we did not raise money, these programs would not continue to exist. The clubs really help kids get off the street and help them stay out of trouble.

I did get a trophy for selling the most day-old newspapers. Of all the trophies I've received (and some are very large ones from the Boy's Club), it is the one I received from Shield's Park that I treasure the most. This one is small in size, but the biggest in my heart and the one I treasured the most.

TOP NEWSBOY—Dan Pistoresi, left, automobile dealer here, is pictured above as he was presented with the Newsboy award by Tony Cortese as the result of selling the most copies of The Independent's special Boys Club edition Tuesday. The presentation was made at last night's annual meeting when $600 was turned over to the club as proceeds of the sale.

We loaned the Moose Lodge cars to get around in during a convention in our area. They gave me a lifetime membership to Moose Heaven, and after I found out that blacks were not allowed, I, in a nice way, turned them down. If I believe in something strongly, I can't be a hypocrite.

AUTOMOTIVE NEWS, OCTOBER 31, 1966

Toyota Dealers Sponsor Sports Broadcast—

Officers of the Northern California Toyota Dealers Advertising Assn. sign a contract for the Thursday night sponsorship of the Sports Report with Ed Hart, over Station KRON-TV in San Francisco. From the left are Gary Wilson, KRON-TV; Dan White, Clinton Frank Advertising; Dan Pistoresi, NCTDAA president; Ottar Dahl, manager of Toyota Dealers, San Francisco; Hil Probert, NCTDAA secretary-treasurer; Tom Freeman, NCTDAA director, and Dick Fedan, NCTDAA vice-president.

For three years straight, I was voted President of the Northern California
Toyota Dealers Advertising Association.

—Independent photo by Prentice Brooks

DOUBLE CHECK—Melody Rambler manager Caesar Perales (left) and sponsor Dan Pistoresi measure the distance between the rubber and home plate that Gary Chaires will be pitching tonight against Vic Joyce and his Reeves Construction nine at Eastshore Park in a Pony League game. Pony hurlers pitch 54 feet, instead of the regulation 60 feet, 6 inches.

Left to right: Caesar Perales, Gary Chaires, and Dan Pistoresi.

SPONSOR—Dan "Mr. Melody Rambler of Richmond" Pistoresi, sponsor of Miss Deborah Hughes, University of California graduate in mathematics; and Mr. J. E. Wyatt, Jr., publisher of Falcon Magazine. Miss Hughes is a leading contestant in the "Miss Falcon" contest, and expects to be present at the "Lady's Dream" pageant at the Oakland Auditorium Theatre September 30.　　　　　—(Evans Photo)

Mr. Melody Rambler of Richmond, California.

MR. MELODY RAMBLER - SPONSERED ONE OF OUR FALCONETTE'S - IN " A LADY'S DREAM" RICHMONDS DAN PISTERESSI - OUTSTANDING PHILARTHROPIST.

Jackie Johnson, Mrs. Carmen, Mrs. Johnson and Nick Nicholson are being interviewed by Cal-Voice W. Moffate.

We sponsored a young lady for the Miss Falcon Beauty Contest.

I heard that Sugar Ray Robinson was fighting Fulmer for the championship in Las Vegas, Nevada, and being a great fan of Sugar Ray Robinson, I wanted to see the fight in the worst way. I called up to get ringside seats. Our tickets were confirmed and we were assigned our seats. I received the four tickets I had ordered. This was terrific.

My friends and I boarded a plane heading to Las Vegas, and when we entered the arena, we headed to our ringside seats. The usher told us that ringside started at Row 10. I was not going to ruin this great night wasting time in arguing. The only bad thing about the fight is that Sugar Ray lost. I lost around $200. After the fight, we went back to the airport and got on a Western Airlines plane headed for home.

After we were in the air for thirty minutes, an engine went out and we had to return to Las Vegas. We were told there would be a three-hour layover, so we headed to the nearest casino, which was at the Hacienda Hotel. When we entered the casino, we saw that a big crowd had gathered at the crap table. A fellow there threw a lot of passes and had a few thousand dollars in front of him. I nudged my way closer to the table to make a wager. The man kept rolling the dice and kept winning. I ended getting my $200 back, and then winning $300 more.

We returned to the airport and again started our trip back to San Francisco. Life is so exciting. There's always something different.

One of our salesmen decided to open up his own used car lot, which I encourage anyone to do. This is what America is like. We all have a chance to try to better ourselves. This particular salesman frequently held a barbecue at his used car lot, and we used to go there for the visit and to eat. We were very good friends. One day this salesman came to see me to say that someone pulled a con job on him and he explained what happened. He had the man and woman arrested. But the way this took place, even if he was right, I did not think he would be able to get a conviction.

I had been on call for jury duty and of all things, when I was called in, it was to sit on the jury for my friend's case. Both attorneys let me stay on. The accused man was a real bad person who had been in trouble many times. His girl was a patient at the Napa Mental Hospital. What he did was make a straw purchase by having his girlfriend sign all the paperwork. However, the dealer did not know she was a mental patient.

After the two lawyers were finished making their cases, we were sent to the jury room. Some of the jurors asked to go back to the court because they did not understand some of the questions. When we returned to the jury room, we got down to the serious business of trying to make the right decision. Guilty, or not guilty. I was having a tough time convincing the other jury members that my friend did not have a case for a conviction, but only one of the jurors was on my side. Most of the jurors wanted to make a fast guilty plea; some said they had other things to do. I really got irritated by what they said. I told them if we have to stay all night to make a decision, then that is what we would do. I said they were basing their guilty verdict on what they knew about the man's background. He really was a bum. But that had nothing to do with the case. It took a good hour of honest discussion to turn them around to a verdict of not guilty.

My friend's attorney asked me why I voted the way I did. I said I did not think my friend had a case. The attorney said that was exactly what he had told his client—that my friend had no chance of winning. Which made me feel good. But disturbed me, was that if I had not been on the jury, the defendant would have been found guilty.

Sitting on a jury is a huge responsibility and should not be taken lightly. Make sure your mind is only on the case you are judging, and be fair when making a decision, even if you happen to know the parties involved. If I knew I was one hundred percent right, I would hate to depend on a jury after the experience I went through while serving on this case.

In the early 1960s, I told my salesmen that because of inflation and taxes in California, we might have to own two houses to have one house free and clear of debt. The taxes California imposed were too high. When you purchased a car and paid your down payment, most of it went for your license plates and taxes. Inflation is the worst thing happening in our country. It makes the rich richer and the poor poorer. Too much inflation will ruin our country more than a war could.

California Has Everything To Offer

California is a beautiful place and it has more to offer than any other state in this country, or in any country in the world. This state has the best weather. You can go snow skiing or surfing, and the beaches are second to none. The fishing here is very enjoyable. It has some of the best restaurants that you would love to dine in. And great scenic adventure sites you can visit, including the famous Disneyland, Knott's Berry Farm, Sea World, and the San Diego Zoo.

Reverend Father Junipero Serra established the missions on the El Camino Real. Don't miss these historic missions. They are a strong part of California's history. A must see! Elaine and I and our children had the pleasure of visiting these places many times, and I really do miss not being able to see them more often.

This state is self-sufficient and could stand on its own and end up with a solid surplus cash flow if it did not have the stupid politicians on both sides of the aisle who have put this great state in a minus equity position. I am not saying that all politicians are bad. But I think 75 percent of them care only for their personal gain, not for the people or the state. The state has to start from scratch and get out of its deep financial hole. So, be careful who you vote for. I do not live in California now, but I still like to visit. Let's keep our money in our great country for a change.

The state of California could really be a country in itself. It has all the natural resources, including oil. It has the best farming land, which makes it one of the top growing states for cotton and the best for producing wine grapes. When my father made wine, he used grapes from California. This state produces the best oranges and grapefruits, and many other fruits, plus a great variety of nuts.

We should all rediscover California. The entire world exists within this one state. If you have never been to California, you are cheating yourself. If you like the desert, you can visit the Mojave Desert. Palm Springs is a very popular spot. San Diego is next door to Mexico, with very nice weather. Avalon, where Catalina Island is located, requires that you take a ship or airplane to get there. It's a beautiful place. The Santa Barbara area and the Sierra Nevada are wonderful. There's Mt. Shasta, Yosemite National Park and so many other exciting places to see and visit. No country in the world offers more to see and enjoy in such a safe environment.

When Elaine and our family lived in California, we attended the old St. Mary's Church in Oakland, California, and became very close friends with Father Kelly. We would have him over to our house for dinner. He baptized one of our children and we stayed very good friends with him until he left this earth. He was strong about the church and yet was still a regular guy. He had that strong Irish wit and Irish principles. He was a hero.

In one of the hotels in Oakland, California, a guest staying there was threatening to commit suicide. The police were there, and so was Father Kelly. While the police were outside of the room, Father Kelly was able to talk the guest out of taking his life. After some time went by, the guest attempted to shoot himself. Father Kelly grabbed the gun and a shot went off. The police broke into the room, but no one had been hurt. Father Kelley had saved a life. Later, I told Father Kelly it seemed he would do anything for publicity. He laughed.

The home we had in El Cerrito, California, was on the tenth hole of Mira Vista Golf Course. I never played on the golf course because I knew I would get hooked on the game. I did play on the municipal course about three times a year and could hit the ball out of bounds from one side to the other, but with a family and a business to run, I figured golf would take too much of my time.

We had a basketball hoop in our backyard, and this way we could all play and enjoy being together. Our friends who visited us liked to play basketball with us. We entertained a lot at home, but when we went out, we would go to our favorite restaurants in San Francisco. The Fairmont Hotel had the greatest lobster thermidor you ever tasted. Fior D Italia's spaghetti used a sauce very close to my mother's recipe, which was second to none. There was also Trader Vics, Vanessi Fleur de Lieu, and some very nice Chinese and Japanese restaurants.

Our house in El Cerrito, California.

Larry and Paul in our El Cerrito house.

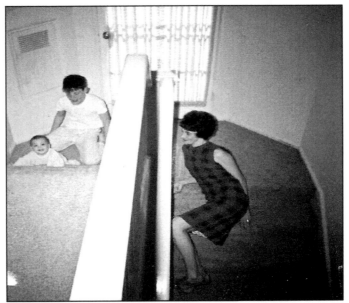

Larry climbing stairs with Michael behind him and Elaine watching.

Danise on left, Larry on right.

Larry on left, Michael in center, Paul on right.

Close to Berkeley, near the railroad tracks, was a great place to get real good seafood. It was called Spengers and they had a fish market next door to the restaurant. They served very good seafood and their deep fried frog legs were out of this world. The frog's legs taste better than chicken. Spengers did so much business that customers did not mind waiting over an hour for seats. The food was worth the wait. The customers would often wait in the bar, and they could be standing four or five deep trying to get a drink.

One day I was sitting by myself and two women were seated at the table next to me. They were talking loud enough that their conversation could be heard at other tables. One woman said to her friend that she should get a divorce from her husband. As they continued talking about the divorce, I got up and went to their table, apologized for overhearing their conversation, and asked if I could say something. They said yes. I asked the woman who was going to divorce how long she had been married. She said 25 years. I asked her if she still loved her husband, and she said yes she did. I asked her if her husband ever stepped out on her before this time and she said no. I did ask her if her husband ever hit her, talked mean, or cussed at her, and she said he never had. I turned to her friend and asked if she was married. The friend replied that she was divorced. "Misery loves company," is what I told her. I turned back to the first woman and said, "Your friend is the last person you should get advice from." I told her that she should talk it out with her husband before making a final decision. This really was none of my business, but from what I heard, it was my moral obligation to try and talk to the person who seemed to be reaching out for help. She thanked me many times. I hope she did not get a divorce.

If you ever have a problem with your marriage and want help and advice, talk to someone who has a happy marriage, or to your minister, so you will have a clear head. Then give it a lot of thought, unless violence is involved. If you have children, make sure that you consider them before you make your final decision. When a divorce happens, the children become the big losers because if both parents remarry and whomever they marry has children, this is where the problems start. In case of a death, and if a lot of money is involved, who will end up with it? There should be a law that in the case of a divorce, children should get a certified claim to the estates of the biological parents. Too many children are left out and end up with nothing. I have seen this happen. This state or federal law should be sponsored by Congress and the senators of every state.

Some children end up with so many stepmothers and stepfathers, stepbrothers and stepsisters that they get lost in the shuffle. This is why it is so urgent that they are not left out when a divorce occurs. Years ago, it was against the law to be cruel to an animal, long before it became against the law to be cruel to a child. When it comes down to the finish line of a divorce, you end up with two stupid people who cannot be in their right mind because they are both blinded by money, lust, greed, selfishness, ignorance, careless about their children, infidelity, and many other stupid excuses. Grow up and snap out of it before you ruin your family and cause so many problems for your children. Your children really have a right to grow up happy with no fears. Over 65 percent of all divorces would not have happened if the two people could have talked things out in an intelligent manner. Of course, with no anger by both parties.

Before any divorce goes forward, both parties should calmly draw a line from top to bottom down the center of a sheet of paper. On one side, list the things you like about your spouse. Then list the things you do not like on the other side. Next, take a little time to get relaxed and refreshed. Check what you wrote earlier and change any items you feel differently about. Feel free to move an item from one side to the other side. Nothing is 100 percent right, but we can all try to get as close as we can to making the right decision.

I am not saying that there should be no divorces ever, because there are many valid reasons for couples separating such as cruelty, violence, continuous fighting, and any form of strong abuse. But before divorcing, this would be the time to take action or try to get some help. Always go back to the question, How did you meet? Was there any indication of the abusive behavior you might not have noticed because you had sex on your mind? Some traits one can sense. When you start to know each other a little better, you will have a chance of having a good married life. You should not step into marriage after knowing each other for just a short time. We all know that everything is not perfect. We spend time to go to school to learn, so why not take the time to learn about the person you might tie the knot with? While you are going together with a person who you think would make a good spouse, and you notice something about that person that irritates you, this is the time you should try to straighten out your problems. If you love each other enough to want to get married and you do not clear things up, your irritations will still be there and your marriage will not last. No one is perfect, so keep a positive attitude to make everything work out. We should enjoy life because it is so beautiful. Smiling more often will make you feel better about everything, including yourself.

Our granddaughter Vanessa and my wife Elaine practicing ballet. Above them is a photo of Vanessa's brother, Joseph, who was run over by a bus.

Keep Healthy And Control Your Weight

This works for me, and I am not suggesting you follow what I am saying, but it won't hurt you to create for yourself some good eating habits. The best way to lose weight is to do it on your own, and it will cost you a lot less money. If you are overweight up to fifty pounds, you do not have to get on any weight loss programs and you do not need to take pills to lose the extra pounds. The simple, and least expensive way, is to eat everything you normally do. For your first four days, fill your plate, but eat slower and leave 25 percent of your food, except your vegetables. Throw what is left in the garbage can. You are not wasting food. You are putting yourself on the way to good health. Starting your fifth day, put less on your plate, eat slowly, and you will get full sooner. The secret is to chew your food longer. This will help your digestive system. You will get tired of chewing and really enjoy the taste of what you are eating.

When you go out to eat and you feel like having a steak and normally you would order that sixteen ounce New York cut, just order the twelve ounce, then eat and chew it slower, and you will get just as full as your normal sixteen ounce and enjoy it more. The next time, get an eight-ounce steak and you will really enjoy it and prove to yourself that you know how to discipline yourself.

The best way to explain how that extra weight slows you down and makes your heart work harder is use the example of racehorses. Suppose one won the race by six lengths, and that one horse finished last by six lengths. Suppose these horses will run on the same track with the same jockeys in two more races. For the winner, add one extra pound of weight, and for the horse that finished last, subtract one pound. The horse that won the race will now win by only two or three lengths, and the one that finished last will end up fourth or fifth. Try this experiment yourself by putting a five-pound weight in your knapsack and walk a mile with it on and you will get tired sooner than you would if you did not have that extra weight. The extra weight takes a toll.

I am not against soda pop, but drinking too much of it is not good for anyone. While our children were growing up, we never let them have soda pop except on rare occasions. We did not have it in the house. Drinking too much soda pop adds extra pounds around your waist. This is why so many kids are overweight. The parents should try to control their children's food and soda intake. This is a very serious problem in our country now and hazardous to the children's future. Our obligation in raising a family is to make it safe for our children, which includes their eating habits and their conduct. I know that not everybody can be thin because some people are going to be on the plump side, but sixty percent of the public is now considered obese.

I love to eat, and when I was growing up and during my time in the maritime service, I could eat two or three helpings at every meal. I never gained a pound, but I did work out and played sports. When I made my homemade spaghetti sauce, I would eat two to three plates full but when I was 26 years old, I noticed I was starting to get a little tire around my waist, and this alert was enough for me to stop eating so much. I was so vain, I did not want any excess fat on me. Putting on excess weight creeps up on us without notice. You can eat the best of foods and still maintain your normal weight.

Your salad dressings can really put on those extra pounds if you use too much. The next time you have salad, just use one teaspoon less dressing, and the next time use two tablespoons less. Mix it thoroughly through the greens and you will enjoy your salad just as much by cutting down on your portions of dressing.

I like most salad dressings, but my favorite is oil and vinegar eaten with hot French bread. I have to make sure I do not eat too much of it. I can make a great satisfying meal with a salad that has a lot of veggies on it. I love a spinach salad, which is very healthy for you. Occasionally, I would go on a seven to 12-day fast without eating, although I drank a lot of water. The first two days are the hardest to do. After the first two days, you are no longer hungry. Once I went 13 days with no food. This is really dumb, but I was testing my endurance. If you go three or four days, it is good for you and your health.

You can really have a lot of fun cutting down on your food consumption by making a game out of it. Buy a scale and weigh yourself every day. You should see a doctor for a check-up and find out if you might need to take certain vitamins for your health. Now everyone is promoting boost drinks and energy drinks, which I think is a waste of money. I do not believe that they help you that much. Stay away from all those types of promotions because no one knows how those products can affect your health. I believe that if you keep a positive attitude and eat right, you will not have to subject yourself to some of these junk drinks that end up costing you a lot of extra money. All these statements are my own opinions that I believe in one hundred percent, and I am not trying to sway anyone, but to caution you before you take that next step.

When you purchase food with an expiration date, make sure you know how much time is left for safe consumption. Large supermarkets do not always pull expired items off the shelf. They are not trying to fool you—most likely, they just missed noticing they should have pulled the product. I am a good shopper and look at everything I buy for an expiration date. Sometimes I find food that has passed its expiration date. I let the storekeepers know and they are usually happy I made them aware of this. Please always check this for your health and welfare. It can save you doctor visits.

I received a call from a dealer friend of mine from Long Beach, California, telling me that his cousin, Ann Francis, was coming to the Bay Area for a couple of days with her husband, Dr. Abeloff. We furnished them with a car, took them to dinner at the Fleur de Lis, and enjoyed a very excellent dinner with our great company. After dinner, we went to see a show at the waterfront. The owner recognized Ann Francis standing in line and wanted us to come right in ahead of everyone. She turned him down to stay in line for her turn. I really admired her for what she did. We enjoyed their company and were very happy that we had a chance to meet them.

While living in the Bay Area, Elaine and I would occasionally go to Reno to gamble and see the shows. American Motors had a get-together at Harold's Club, the most popular casino in Reno. Ray Sutton, Bill Wilson, another fellow, and I were all playing at the craps table and we were on a winning streak. It rarely happens, but we were all throwing a lot of sevens and elevens. We walked away with over $5,000 each. Harold Smith Jr., a terrific guy, had been watching us play. He gave me an autographed copy of his book and we started talking. Coin collecting came up and I told him that it was a hobby of mine. He said I should talk with his son and set up a meeting. When they came to see me, we talked about coin collecting and the son said that if I were interested in collecting silver dollars he would sell me some. Each bag held 1,000 silver dollars. I knew some coin dealers in Reno and they could not buy them from Harold's Club. So I would buy four to six bags at a time and his staff would load them into the trunk of my car and escort me out of town in case someone might be following.

Trini Lopez was playing at Harold's Club when we were there. Harold Smith Jr. asked me if I would like to see the Trini Lopez show with my family. I was very happy with his offer. He said there was one obstacle, which was that I would need to sit behind the post in the showroom. We were enjoying the Trini Lopez show and in comes Harold Smith Jr. He wanted to make sure I followed orders. He was so nice to me and a very easy person to talk to.

One Sunday, we went to the Catholic Church in Reno and when it was time to pass the collection basket, they handed one to me to my surprise. I was collecting the offerings and about halfway up the aisle I saw Harold Smith Jr.'s son, the one who had sold me silver dollars. When I got to where he was sitting, he gave me a smile. He was with his family. Afterwards, when we walked out of church, he came up to me and said, I guess they trust everybody.

Rose Sum with her sister, our dear friend Father J.J. Kelly, and my wife Elaine at our home celebrating the adoption of our son Lawrence J. Pistoresi.

The Privilege Of Adopting Children

We had always intended to adopt at least two children. Our friend, Dr. Paul Ryan, lived across the street from us in El Cerrito, California, and we told him we would like to adopt two children. He told us he had a birth coming up. On May 14, 1962, we had the pleasure of getting a little boy. His name is Lawrence John Pistoresi. We were able to get him at the age of two days old. When you are lucky enough to be able to adopt a child, you will get such a great thrill and a great happy feeling that is like a miracle in your life. On January 1, 1964, Dr. Ryan presented us with adoption of another little boy named Paul Joseph Pistoresi. We received him at the age of five days old.

We took them at birth and did not want to know the parents. The reason for this is that if you do not know, you raise the child in your own environment because they are your own children and you are responsible for their health and welfare. The adopted child is not a toy. He or she is your family and shares your name and the same love you give to the rest of the family.

The people who give up their child to be adopted should not have the right to find out who adopted them. Their later involvement would tend to disrupt a child and can have a psychological effect during their growing years. It will also disrupt the adopted parents' life, which can cause a lot of other serious problems, mostly for the child. In emergency situations, such as if an adopted child develops a rare disease, the doctors might need a

DNA match with the biological parents. In such a case, the doctor should be allowed to seek out the mother or the father of the child.

Before we were lucky to be able to have children, we took care of our nieces when they were very young and while they were growing up. They would come to live with us on and off, and when they were picked up, we hated to part with them, even though we were not their parents. They were part of our family and we really did not want to let go. Their mother was having a hard time raising them, and we were happy to be there to help as much as we could. It is hard to detach yourself. They had a very nice mother and she did a very nice job in raising her daughters. The girls turned out to be great mothers, and all of them have great husbands and wonderful children.

We have always let our adopted sons know we were very lucky to be able to adopt them. As they got older, we told them that if they want to find out who their parents were, they had our blessing. So far, they do not want to know. The door is open if they want to seek them out. This is only their choice and not the parents' choice. They already gave up their rights when they let the children be legally adopted.

Some friends called us when we were living in California and said they had a very serious problem. I said, "I hope you are not getting a divorce." They said, no, but their daughter was pregnant. We told them not to let their daughter get an abortion. We suggested she stay with us until she gave birth. When she had her child, we got her a dozen roses. She gave the baby up for adoption, which saved a life and made another family happy. And I mean very happy.

I always helped changed diapers for all our children. The husband should always help with the children. When Elaine and I decided we needed extra help, we didn't want to just get a babysitter because you never know who you are really getting. The safety of our children was a priority, so we decided to hire a live-in nanny. Her name was Ann Jones and she did no housework or cooking. Her husband was a radio operator on Merchant ships, and her son, Tom Jones, was at officer's training at West Point or Annapolis. He also flew with the Blue Angels or Flying Thunderbirds. She liked my cooking and suggested I open a restaurant and write a book.

My wife and I had to go to Portland, Oregon, and while we were there, we received a call from Ann that Larry was sick and his face was swollen. We went back home and took him to the hospital to find out that he had Nephritic Syndrome and they put him on Prednisone, a very strong controlled substance that would have to be tapered off as he improved. This went on for a few years. His face would swell so much that he could hardly see. It also stunted his growth. At the age of fifteen, his bones were that of a ten-year-old. As of this writing, he is in his late forties and still lives at home. He taught himself to paint and has sold a lot of his paintings. He also makes intricate things out of plastic. We think he is a genius and so do a lot of other folks who know him. He would be a very good pattern maker with his ability. He tried to get a job with George Lucas.

Our CPA, Glen Whalen, had a friend who wanted to sell cars, so Glen asked if I would give him a job. I hired Carl, who had a wife and child. After working for us for about six months, he was accused of molesting a child. The story made the papers. I was a witness at his hearing and I said he should be put in jail. If they let him go, he should have a right to earn a living or he would be a menace to society. I would not let him work for us anymore. I believe he should have been locked up for a long time.

I decided to sell my 75-percent interest in the San Bruno auto dealership to Bill Wilson, who owned the other 25 percent. This was a real moneymaker, located in San Bruno, California, a very good area. During the transaction, I told our CPA to make sure there was a bank audit each month. Ed Holmes was the business manager and Glen Whalen was the CPA for all of our dealerships, and I had let him buy into our Casa De Chrysler dealership in Richmond.

I have let my ego get in the way of my common sense at times. At that point, I was trying to grow too fast. I wanted 13 dealerships. But none of that was because of personal greed. It was about how much good we could accomplish with the money we made to help those in need. I did overspend on entertainment. At that time, money was easy to borrow.

When I was fourteen years old, I had worried about my father because he worked so hard for the little he made, yet he was able to buy a house and made sure we ate well. My dad and mother were very good cooks and that made a lot of difference; we always had food on the table. But it was hard to get a little ahead to have something for emergencies that came up. This situation really woke me up and I vowed not to be in the same position my father had been in. I set a goal that before I was 40 years old, I would have at least $100,000 in cash. I did not have a plan to start my endeavor, but I did have 26 years to accomplish it. When I was 39, I had a very good net worth. The only reason that I sold the San Bruno, California, dealership was to accomplish my 26-year old goal, which I did. I am not taking all the credit because if it were not for my wonderful wife behind me, this might not have happened. And, of course, having very good employees helped.

The goals that you set for yourself could be for anything you desire or might want to do. The most famous goal I accomplished was to have a great wife and a great family. Plus, you are only as strong in business as your employees make you.

I am not smart. I was just an average student in school and I am not really a writer. This book has been a goal of mine for 35 years. After this goal, my next goal is to get back into the restaurant business. And the goal after that will be to celebrate my 110th birthday. With this goal, I will need God's help.

Life is very beautiful. Remember one thing: that we all have our ups and downs. Just never give up. We all have to keep a positive attitude and to try to smile a little more. If you smile, you will feel much better about yourself and the world that you live in.

The one thing that everyone—and I mean everyone—should learn is how to cook, at least a little bit because as you grow older, knowing how to cook will come in handy and save you a lot of money. Some schools have Home Economics courses and you can get a good idea about how to cook there. Most boys thought taking Home Economics was kind of sissy when I was growing up. But some of those people became very good chefs and made a lot of money doing what they enjoyed.

End Of The World

The end of the world does come many times in our lifetime. Just think about it. When an earthquake happens, or if you drown, or if you get shot and die, or perhaps get killed in war, or you die in a fire, it is the end of the world for you. My own opinion is that man will destroy the world before the world comes to an end and we've had a great start to accomplish this if we do not snap out of it. The degenerate molesters hurting our children and drugs are causing people to become weak. We have to be more severe with everybody that hurts our children.

After selling San Bruno, I decided to invest many thousands of dollars in American Express, Jefferson Insurance, and IBM, and I lost thousands of dollars on these stocks. I did break even on Jefferson Insurance.

Just after selling San Bruno, I was in a car with my business manager, Ed Holmes. I handed him an envelope and asked him to count it. Then I told him the $5,000 in cash was for him. He started to get tears in his eyes. I said I appreciated him for being an excellent business manager and for being my friend. He had polio and it crippled him to the point that he could hardly walk. He used a cane to get around.

While we were in Richmond, I tried to locate some of the friends I had grown up with. Michael Galvin was one of the pals I ran around with. We went to the same high school and worked at Iron Fireman, and at Northern Pacific Railroad as firemen together.

I found out he was in the Roseburg, Oregon, Veterans Administration Rehab Hospital. I called the hospital to see if I could visit Michael and was told I could. I flew from San Francisco to Medford, Oregon, then rented a car and drove to the hospital in Roseburg. It sure was nice to see him and we had a great visit. I asked him if he would like to come and visit us. I set up a meeting with the staff to ask if there was anything about Michael I needed to be aware of. I hadn't seen him for 20 years and a lot could happen to change a guy during that time.

I met with two nurses, two doctors, and the Hospital Administrator. Some of the questions were directed at alleviating any worries I might have concerning the safety of my children. One nurse said he always giggled and I said he'd always been that way. I asked if there was anything else. The nurse said that once he had given her a bouquet of flowers. I asked if he had made any advances toward her, tried to touch her, talk dirty to her, or played with himself in front of her. She answered that he had never done any of that. However, she said they had placed him on detention because she had misunderstood what he had meant when he gave her the flowers. I told the nurse he had just been expressing his gratitude for how she had taken care of him. He had been a patient there a long time. I made arrangements to come and pick him up to take him to our home in California.

When we arrived in San Francisco, he wanted to be on his own for a few days, so I put him up at the Jack Tar Hotel. I told the desk clerk to let him order whatever he wanted. When I returned the next morning to pick him up, he had five cartons of cigarettes, three boxes of cigars, and four boxes of chocolates. I had to laugh. Later, I took him to my home and let him stay with us for a while. He said he wanted to work for me at the dealership, and I told him he could if he wanted to. He asked what the pay would be and I said he would make $1,000 a month. He said he wanted a management position, and I said that after he'd worked awhile, and if he was qualified, he might have a chance at a promotion. His response was that he couldn't afford to work for me. I couldn't believe what I was hearing. He explained that he received over $400 a month, banks $400 each month, has free room and board, transportation, access to a tennis court, his medical care is covered and he doesn't have to work a day. He said that once or twice a week he sneaks out to one of the local taverns for a night of fun, drinking beer, and dancing.

Michael mentioned that some of the psychiatrists who treat the patients end up in the hospital themselves. When a new doctor is hired, the patients bet on how long it will take until he becomes a patient. Not all of them end up as patients, but some do.

After hearing all this, I had to agree that he was better off where he was. He had become comfortable with his surroundings and I felt I would do him more harm than good by trying to move him out.

When we were growing up, Michael and I were very close pals. He was a terrific baseball pitcher as a kid. He could have played high school ball, but chose not to. A lot of talent went along the roadside because the kids made a choice not to participate, for whatever reason. That was their choice. But now that we were grown, I was concerned about Michael's health and welfare. It's so sad how we change as we grow up. The years pass too quickly and all of a sudden, you are not a child anymore.

We were taught right and wrong from our parents and sometimes we were taught the wrong way from our teachers. And I am speaking of at least 40 percent of teachers nowadays are not teaching our children what they should be learning. Teachers now, in most cases, are confused about what life is really about. I do not like the way they teach because they don't know how. I am not saying all teachers are bad, because of course a lot of them are excellent teachers who went into teaching for the right reasons. For the ones who influence young children into not respecting our great country, this caliber of a teacher should go to another country to live and teach the way they think.

If you can afford to send your children to a Christian school, you will have a better chance for your child to get the right education. I am not against public schools because I have attended two of them. I will say that I did learn more from a Catholic school than I did from two public schools. This is my own observation, thinking for myself. When it comes time that we cannot think for ourselves, we are all going to be in a lot of trouble. Always think positive and be your own person. This will make you a great person and a strong citizen of your great country. While growing up, and through this very day, I am so proud I could pledge allegiance to the United States of America and to know the preamble to the United States and the Gettysburg Address. When we see the evil going on around us, we must get stronger as individuals to protect our country.

When Ray Sutton was working for me, he asked me if I would hire his father. I told him I would be very happy to hire his father. His father worked for us for about three months, but then started to get homesick for Ohio. Ray's wife, Marcy, was a great seamstress and made all her beautiful clothes. They had two children, Tom and Cindy. Ray decided to open up a used car lot in Sacramento and I was very happy for him. He had a real beautiful car lot and was doing very well. A few months later, he was starting to go downhill and quickly went bankrupt. I felt sorry for him losing it all. He ended being out of a job and asked me if I would hire him back. I did hire him back.

Bank of America advised me that I should not hire him back. I asked them why. They said that they could not make that disclosure. I did hire him back anyway. That was the fourth time I hired Ray Sutton. He worked for us for a few months, then went back to Sacramento.

My CPA wanted me to hire back Carl Magno and I would not do it. When a person is convicted of a molestation crime, I cannot stand being around such a creature. It would bother me too much. This did not sit too well with my CPA and it did not help our business relations. When you have your strong convictions, no one should try to sway you. Stand up for what is morally right.

Carl Magno went back to Seattle to work for his brother who had a used car lot. I wanted to expand to Novato, California, to open another location. I went to Novato to check out a number of locations to see if I could put all of this together. I found one parcel on an acre of land that I thought would make a suitable location. I already had the letter of intent from Toyota and Chrysler Corp.

I knocked on the door of the house that sat on this property. The owner came to the door. I introduced myself to her and explained why I wanted to buy her property. She told me that she was born in that house 52 years ago and had no intention of moving. I told her I would like to come back to see her the next day and talk to her again, even if she decided not to move. I did set up an appointment to see her the following day. During our meeting, she decided to tear down her house and build me a new car showroom and garage so we could open up our dealership. This property was just below McGraw Hill Publishing Company. The owner gave me a twenty-year lease and sold me two commercial lots next to the old post office. Three months later, she called me up and said she had just realized what she did, and was now living in an apartment. I told her that in the long run she would end up with a great investment. I did not put up one cent, or the first or last month's rent. I paid only the first month to start the opening. The owner was a very nice person and honored every detail of our lease.

I strongly believe that when you are in any business, you should do all you can and everything you can afford to help your community. You can make this a real fun thing, and if you can get everybody into the act, it will not cost each individual business very much. I tried to get my fellow dealers to get involved, but they were not interested.

Our dealership sponsored the Richmond High School baseball team during the summer vacations so that they could stay in shape. When you show that you really support the youths, they will respect what you do for them. When they grow to adulthood, they will still remember what you did for the community. Always use your good judgment when conducting business.

I was pressured into selling our beautiful Novato dealership. This was like having a gold mine stolen from you. I created dealerships in locations where none had been. The person that ended with my Toyota dealership was a bank customer. When you try to expand too much and have to cut down on your operation, vultures wait on the sidelines for a chance to get something they did not have the ability to do on their own.

My empire was getting smaller and smaller and I decided to move my Toyota Richmond dealership to my Chrysler Plymouth dealership next door. Everything was going smoothly. Then before I knew it, I realized I was going out of business. My cash flow was low. Money from the bank is easy to get when you do not need it. The time I really needed it was right then, and all of a sudden, no money was to be had. The bank doors were closed to me.

To be on the record, I explained to the IRS that if I could sell my Toyota franchise and keep the money, it would help me a lot. To my surprise, they approved my selling of the franchise and keeping the money I received. I really appreciated what they did for me. But then I was out of work and had to find a new position. When I've had to work for others, I've been very fussy about who I will work for.

My first choice was Mike Salta, who I had worked for before. My second choice was Herb Bidulph, who I knew in Las Vegas. My third choice was to work for my pal Frank Antonacci, who I had grown up with. I called Mike Salta and he hired me. I went to Long Beach, California, for a while, then to Costa Mesa to check things out. While I was there, Rock Hudson's mother came to the dealership and purchased a Chrysler Three Hundred. I had a chance to talk to her, and she said she was real worried about her son, Rock Hudson. I felt sorry for her and her son. I was in Costa Mesa for just a short time, and from there I went to Redlands, California, to check out a dealership. Redlands is where many movie stars had their summer homes and getaways. Elaine and I leased a beautiful old home that sat on over 25 acres of oranges, grapefruit, figs, avocados, and other trees.

I can see why Hollywood stars choose Redlands for their summer homes. It is really a nice place to live. We had a large, deep swimming pool and a large yard for picnics and entertaining friends. We bought two Appaloosa horses for Michael and Danise, who had all the room in the world to ride and enjoy themselves. Larry and Paul were too young to ride at that time. The Loma Linda Hospital was two miles away and it is a very great hospital, second to none. We took our son Larry there for his treatments. We were really enjoying Redlands and figured we would live there for some time. Michael and Danise went to high school in Redlands and liked it very much.

One day, our dear friend Herb Bidulph paid me a visit and explained what had happened to Cal Popejoy, their general sales manager, who had been sent to prison at Terminal Island for the illegal selling of paint franchises. He had been selling the same franchise to more than one person and was sentenced to a minimum two-year stretch. Herb wanted me to see his dealership so I could determine if I was interested in joining him there.

I took my son Michael with me and Herb laid out an offer. His worksheet showed I would have an 11-percent ownership, the same percentage that had been given to Cal Popejoy. Cal had been with Herb for a long time and he was like a father to him. This offer was hard to turn down and I told Herb I would accept.

This next thing I had to do, which was difficult for me, was to call Mike Salta, my friend. My wife and I are godparents to some of his children, so telling him what I was about to do was painful. I said our son Larry would be needing a lot of medical treatments and that I would be getting an 11-percent ownership as a sign on. Mike Salta wished me the best.

I went to Las Vegas and started work as the general sales manager for Herb Bidulph. I found myself in an uncomfortable situation because most of the salesmen had worked under Cal for many years and I was a new face coming in as their boss. I understood how they felt, and worked hard to gain their acceptance and trust. Finally, everything was running smoothly and we developed into a great sales force.

With the help of some of the salesmen and Cal's brother Bob, a house to live in was picked out for us. Bob knew the owner. He talked to his friend and told her I was interested in buying her house. Bob and I took the owner to dinner to talk to her and make a deal for her house. After dinner, I got out a yellow legal-sized paper and wrote up a contract. She was in a great hurry to get her furs out of storage and to catch a plane heading back east to meet up with her sugar daddy. She told us she had two sugar daddies, one on the west coast, and the one she would be visiting on the east coast. She said they were heading for Venezuela.

I mentioned to her that since she flew a lot, I would take out some insurance on her since I was buying her house. She said she would deal with that when she got back. One week later, the plane she was on en route to Venezuela crashed and all aboard were killed. This made me feel so sad. I had just moved my family from Redlands into our new home in Las Vegas. I am very happy that I had the signed contract on the house.

I found out later that the woman's sister had a shirttail ownership of five percent in the house we had purchased. This was a fiasco, so we had to work out a new agreement where my family would have free rent until we found another house to buy.

One day at the car dealership, the foreman for Wayne Newton's ranch came in to buy a used Jeep for the ranch. Later in the day, Wayne Newton came into my office, put out his hand to shake mine, and thanked me for the sale. Outside of my best pleasure of meeting Ethel Barrymore, Wayne Newton was my second best pleasure of stars I have met. He is a very terrific person and a gentleman. Very nice and down to earth. He asked me if I would like to see his show. I was delighted at the offer and he let me bring eight guests to his dinner show. We had so much fun enjoying his terrific performance.

At that time, Las Vegas did not have a large population and the casinos catered to the town's residents. We could get a very large—and I mean a VERY large—shrimp cocktail with all the crackers you could eat, for fifty cents. "A meal in itself," the menu boasted.

I learned that Cal Popejoy had been let out of prison, a year or two earlier than expected. After he was out for a few days visiting with his wife and family, he came back to work. Now we had two general managers to lead. I have to say that this was a lot easier to do than one would expect. Cal and I got to be very good friends and we respected each other.

Cal and I would take turns closing at night. I heard a rumor that Herb was going to sell the dealership. I told Cal about the rumor, and he said he did not know about it; Herb had never said anything to him about selling the dealership. This was all hush-hush and Cal was irritated that Herb had not mentioned anything to him about selling. After work, we would go to a club near the dealership to play pool and have a drink. I was going to be off that night, but just before leaving for the club to play pool, Cal asked if I would trade nights with him. If I would work that night, he would work the next night. So that night I stood in for him, which I was happy to do. About an hour later, I received a call that someone had robbed the club and that Cal had been shot and killed by the perpetrator. This was a terrible tragedy. Cal had been home for just a short time. If we had not traded nights, I would have been the one remaining at the club. My life had been spared again.

A little while after the funeral, Herb Bidulph did sell the dealership to Fratto and Mazzola. They had never owned a new car dealership before and brought in with them a used car manager who was a real jerk. Now we had three confused individuals. Since they kept me, I told them that the person they brought with them was not qualified for the job. I said I knew someone who would be a good used car manager for them. They brought the guy in to talk with, but were not sure they wanted him. Fratto and Mazzola said something came up on the man's background search, but they decided to go ahead and hire him. This was the fifth time I hired Ray Sutton.

My very good friend, Carlo Apa, who was also my insurance agent, decided to come visit us. He and his wife Charlotte had left Reno and were on their way to our home when he passed away. I went to Portland, Oregon, to help bury him. He was only 52 years old. He was a friend who would visit my folks to make sure they were okay. They were very nice friends.

While I am at the funeral, I was fired from my job. When I came back to work, I told them they could have waited until I got back to fire me instead of doing it by phone. I said the way they were running their dealership, they would be out of business within one year. I think they lasted eighteen months. I did not wish them bad luck, but they should have stayed in the used car business. They were really out of their league.

I went to the Lincoln Mercury dealership and the owner hired me as the used car manager. I told Jersey, the general manager, I was going to take an inventory of the used cars, and he said that it was not necessary. To me, this rang an alarm, and I was determined to take an inventory. I could not account for 22 used cars that showed up as being in stock. I was responsible, so I decided to tell the owner we were short thousands of dollars worth of cars I could not account for. He told me that Jersey had been with him for a long time and he would not do anything wrong. "End of story," he said.

While I was there, I met one of the Ink Spots, who had purchased a Lincoln and was dropping it off for service. Later that evening, a young lady was driving out with his car, and after she passed me, she backed up and said, "Don't you remember me?" She said she was Florette, and that I had purchased an evening gown for her in Richmond, California. She was married to one of the members of the Ink Spots, a vocal group, and she invited me to their house on the golf course.

One of my employees told me a pizza business was for sale across from the Sahara Hotel. I ended up buying the pizza business, which was called Pizza King. Art Carney came into our pizza shop and I was happy to meet him. We did get a lot of show people who came in to get pizza. We had slot machines in our place. I did not realize until much later that my background, back to my school days, had been checked before I was approved for a gambling license.

A year later, Jersey and the business manager were caught stealing from the owner of the Lincoln Mercury dealership. He had not believed me when I told him what was happening with the missing inventory. Whenever you get hired as a manager, no matter what type of business, you must keep track of your inventory because you could be set up by even the owner. This has happened a few times. Always protect yourself when you are in management. Before you can be hired as a salesman in Nevada, you will have to be checked out. We had three people who wanted to sell cars for us. One of them was a bank robber, one was a con man, and one was a cattle rustler. Of the three men applying for the job, only one of them was a man we could not hire—the cattle rustler.

The lounge shows in Las Vegas are good at every casino. The Frontier Hotel had Frank Sinatra, Jr. playing there and we went to see him. We decided to go to the dining lounge to get something to eat. While eating, Frank Sinatra, Jr. walks in and goes to a table of four, shakes their hands, and talks to them for a little while. Then he came over to our table to greet us. This is how we met him. He was friendly and a very nice person.

When Marty Robbins was playing, we went to hear him many times. He had so much talent. We had a chance to meet him and talked to him for a few minutes. He was a very easy person to talk to. My wife and some of our friends who had seen his show really loved him. We are all sorry that he passed away at such a young age. While we lived in Las Vegas, we did get to see some of the greatest talent and were able to meet some of them. We learned that most of them are very nice and polite.

When I was at our pizza restaurant, I received a call from Bill Wilson, who was still a minor partner of mine. I had helped him get the financing together for his own car dealership, and let him buy me out of my Rambler dealership in San Bruno, California. I helped him get a Toyota franchise. I did this for him even though he tried to beat me out of $5,000 from the sale that I made to him. I told Bill that I knew he was not calling me to ask about my health. I said, "Now, Bill, what type of problem are you having?" He said his business manager had come up short $125,000. I really felt very sorry for him to get beat out of that kind of money in the 1970s.

When I sold the dealership to Bill, I had told the CPA, Glen Whalen, that Bill Wilson should get a bank audit each month so he would know where he stands. Bill wanted to know if I would be willing to come to San Francisco to be a witness. I told him that I would, but I would have to say he tried to beat me out of $5,000. I have never held a grudge against anyone. Bill had a tough chance of winning against some of the high dollar attorneys with their office in the Trans America building in San Francisco. And I had a moral obligation to try to help Bill. I was his long shot in winning.

When I arrived in San Francisco, both the CPA Glen Whalen, and Bill Wilson could not do enough for me. I could have made a lot of side money if I was on the take. There was $125,000 at stake, plus some high dollar fees. Just before we were to appear in court, both parties indicated they wanted to wine and dine me. But the only thing I wanted from both parties was for them to split my expenses, which were minimal. I could have held them for a lot more money, but I did not want to do it. This made me feel much better about myself.

The CPA's bonding company, with their high-priced attorneys, was there to defend Glen Whalen against a malpractice suit filed by Bill Wilson.

When I was put on the stand, the bonding company's attorney started to badger me, and after a few questions, he tried to make me out as a liar. He asked me if I would be willing to take a polygraph test. I told the attorney I would be happy to. Before you start taking the test, you are asked to lie in response to one question so they can see what happens on their machine when you lie. I do not remember the question they asked, but it could have been, Does two and two equal four? and I would have said, no. After being asked a lot of questions and the test was finished, the person who administered the test asked me what my feelings were about the case. I told him I just wanted to tell the truth. Glen Whalen had to take the polygraph test, too. I passed and he failed the test.

Bill Wilson received his money and if it were not for me, he would have lost his case. The bonding company's attorneys had been sure they would win. They thought they had the win in the bag. I found this out when I went to get my reimbursement for their half of my expenses. Their attorney told me they had given Glen Whalen a polygraph test to see if they had a case and he had passed their test. They said they would have had a better chance of winning if they had not given me the test. The high-powered attorneys were flabbergasted they lost. They are not very nice when you are sitting on the stand. They go right for your throat.

The food business was always on my mind. One day, I went to one of the Pizza Hut Restaurants in Las Vegas and found they really did serve a good pizza. I noticed that they had a pan on a burner that had tomato sauce in it, and I told them it was unsanitary and they should stop doing it that way.

I asked the manager of that location if I could bring him some of my spaghetti sauce and some lasagna, to taste. I thought Pizza Hut might like my concept. When I came back with the samples, they said the sauce and lasagna were terrific.

N

Tonight Show   NBC Television Network Division   3000 West Alameda Avenue
National Broadcasting Company, Inc.   Burbank, CA 91523   213-845-7000, 849-3911

May 15, 1978

Mr. Dan Pistoresi
18880 South Central Point Rd.
Oregon City, Oregon 97045

Dear Mr. Pistoresi:

Mr. Carson asked me to write and thank you
for your kind comments and for your offer
to prepare lasagna for him.

He appreciates your thoughtfulness but must
decline your offer.

Thank you for your interest and kind thought.

Sincerely,

Drue-Ann Wilson
Assistant to
Mr. Johnny Carson

The manager suggested I contact Hal Taylor, who was the head of their commissary at their headquarters in Wichita, Kansas. I called Hal Taylor, told him about my idea, and said I thought it would work very well for them. Hal was interested and I sent him a gallon of spaghetti sauce and a large lasagna to sample. Hal liked my products and asked me if I would like to work out some arrangements to promote my concept. My lasagna could be easily cooked in the pizza ovens without any change in temperature. This meant no new equipment expense and no confusing changes in procedures. But, as we were working things out, a small company named Pepsi bought out Pizza Hut. This was my damper.

I sold the Pizza King restaurant and decided to go to Preferred Equities developing in Pahrump, Nevada. Our office was in the Circus Circus Casino. I sat at the tables trying to convince people to purchase part of the Pahrump property. A person really could not lose on this investment with a small down payment, low interest rates, and six months to a year to make a final decision to keep it. We would comp prospects with two nights and three days and tickets to some of the top shows playing in town. We would take them out to see the property they reserved. This way, the prospective buyers could make up their minds if they wanted to purchase the property, and if they did not want the property, they would get their money back, with ease.

The owners of the property in Pahrump, Nevada, had already developed land in Florida. They were very good at what they were doing. After I was there a couple of months, they made me their public relations manager. I had two suites of rooms in the Circus Circus Casino, with a bar and furniture to greet the people who decided to take on our program. Instead of waiting six months to one year to go see the property, I was there to try and convince them to look and inspect the property the very next day. If they would agree, I would give them extra tickets to different shows. I would tell them it would take as long as ten to twenty years before anything would be built there. If they thought that might not work for them, it might work for their children or for their grandchildren.

During our breaks, I would watch the circus acts, which were marvelous. I mentioned to the person next to me that I enjoyed the acts very much. He said he did too. The man turned out to be Bob Newhart and I shook hands with him. He sure was a down-to-earth person.

The buffet lunch at the Circus Circus was out of this world. The company paid for our lunches, so we would be close by at all times.

When we would put on our program, we would all stand in line inside our room. The customers would stand in line outside our door. When the doors opened, we would greet our specific couple and take them to our table to get as much information as we could before our podium speaker was ready to start the program. After the pitch was made, we would try to talk our customers into taking on our program. When a couple decided to join up with us, they would end up in my suite of rooms so I could talk to them.

I closed a lot of sales for the company, but felt they were not paying me enough for my efforts. So, I resigned and went over to Landex, which had property located close to the Grand Canyon where the Colorado River flows into Lake Mead. It is awesome to look at the Grand Canyon. You can turn your head, look back, and it will look different. You will never get tired of looking at it because it is always different. We would fly our customers to the property and sometimes we would take them through the Grand Canyon and fly just eighty feet above the Colorado River. This was very thrilling and exciting to all of us on the plane.

When I was in Las Vegas, I was in need of some dental work and asked a friend if he knew a dentist in Las Vegas. He told me he went to Tijuana, Mexico, for his dental work. My friend gave me the name and phone number so that I could make an appointment with the dentist to have him work on me. I was told the dentist had attended a dental college in California. I drove my limo to Tijuana and parked it on the California side and walked across the border to see the dentist. He was a very sharp looking man. The work I needed was going to take a couple days, so I checked into a hotel and he started to work on me. After the first session, I went back to my hotel and had a few shots of Haig and Haig pinch bottle, which is my favorite scotch. The dentist really did a very nice job on my teeth.

I always bought Mexican cigarettes whenever I was in Mexico. When I was heading back over the border, going through customs, I had my cigarette in hand and I was looking all over for an ashtray but could not find one, so I went to the restroom and dumped it into the toilet and then went through customs. The custom officer asked me a lot of questions. He said to go to his office, and when I was in there, another person came in. They searched me all over and asked me to strip down to my shorts. I was getting nervous and scared. Then they had me loosen my shorts. After this terrible ordeal was over and I got dressed, I asked them why I had to go through this type of search. They said they saw me moving around and looking suspicious. I told them that I'd just had dental work done and it had taken two days. I told them I was looking for an ashtray and that it would be a good idea to have some around.

In my opinion, the reason the customs officers treated me the way they did was because I had a limo with Illinois plates. This limo had been owned by a felon and had been seized by the FBI.

The very next morning, back in Las Vegas, I parked my limo in town. When I returned to the limo, I noticed a note on my windshield saying, "Honey, please call me." The note included a name and the woman's phone number. I did not make the call, but I could not get to DMV fast enough to register the limo in my name. The person I had purchased the limo from was a lawyer in Los Angeles.

Back at my job, I sat at the tables selling lots in Meadview, Arizona. It was the kind of deal as we had in Pahrump, except that Meadview was all laid out and had some commercial buildings up already. A few people were living there. They had water tanks that held thousands of gallons of the best tasting water I've ever drunk. They had a few miles of paved roads. A little later, I was put in charge of public relations. We all had to have a real estate license to sell property in Arizona. Permanent trailers or manufactured homes were the best housing for the area. The property was sold at a very fair low price starting at $3,500 per lot. This was very good property for people who wanted to retire or own a vacation home to get away from it all. The climate had a perfect temperature and you could grow just about everything you could want.

With my Cadillac limo, I could take more people to the airport to fly to Meadview to show the property. I would make two round-trips just about every day. Joseph Hutchins was the general manager and he was top-notch. The property owners were super nice people. This was a real fun and exciting job. This job made me feel great because I knew I was doing a great favor for the customers who were interested in purchasing the property.

Some of the people that I closed the deal with lived on the East Coast. After they had been home for a couple of months, I would send them a layout of all our property and let them know when a lot next to their property was available and suggest they buy it. The customers were happy that I would let them know and would often purchase their second lot from me. When there was no lot open for sale next door to theirs, I would tell them about other lots that were open, and I sold a lot more property this way. This alone tells you that this property was a terrific buy.

I really would high pressure the young married couples because I knew I was doing them a favor. And sometimes they were a hard sell. I explained that inflation would make it harder for young people to purchase property. I feel very good when I can give common sense advice to others.

Elaine and I had just purchased a new house and had only been living in it a short while when I received a call from my friend Frank Antonacci that a mutual friend of ours needed a general manager for his car dealership in Oregon City, Oregon. At that time, we were taking care of my mother-in-law because we did not want her in a nursing home. She had lost control of her colon and had a hard time walking. Our youngest sons, Larry and Paul, did an outstanding job in helping to take care of their grandmother.

That was one move I hated to make. The people I worked for were very nice and made my work easy. But having both sides of our families getting up in age helped us to make up our minds to move back to the Portland area.

I accepted the job as general manager on the terms that I would have complete control of the sales force; otherwise, they did not need me. After our breakfast, with the factory rep attending, the owner mentioned that I was there to help them. When I got up to say my two cents, I told the staff that I was the general manager and they would no longer be taking their problems to the owner. I would be handling all future problems. Only if we are unable to settle the problem, would we go to the owner together. I told them all that I would take 10 percent of the credit when we did well and 100 percent of the blame when we did not do well. You can only have one person in charge.

Elaine and I sold our house in Las Vegas and purchased a house in Oregon City. We also purchased some adjoining acreage to accommodate future plans.

The owner had a son, a real terrific young man, who worked in the office. The owner's daughter was a very sweet young lady who had polio and had a hard time getting around. I had a little misunderstanding with the owner because he shorted me a few hundred dollars, which eventually he did square with me. This created some hidden bad feelings. Shortly afterwards, when the owner was at a convention out of state, his son asked me to go to breakfast with him. After we ate, he said he was ready to take over my position. He said they no longer needed my service and was acting on his father's instructions. I do not know how this real nice young man could make such a decision when it took him five minutes to figure out what he wanted on his hamburger. I sincerely felt sorry for him because he was way out of his league. He lasted only a few months at the dealership, then gave it up. The only thing that bothered me about all of this was that the father was not the one to fire me, or even to tell me that we could no longer work together. If he would have done this like a gentleman, I would not have cared so much. Even though the owner of the dealership was weak, I still liked him.

Frank Antonacci had just bought into the oldest Ford dealership in Portland. Frank was the general manager, and I was hired as the general sales manager. My father purchased two Model T Fords from Francis Ford. My wife's brother, Joe, purchased a car from us. Three months later, a policeman came to the dealership to ask if I knew about a particular car because it had a lot of overdue parking tickets. It turned out to be the car my brother-in-law bought from us. He lived in an apartment close by and when the policeman went to locate him, they found him murdered. He had been stuffed into a plastic bag with his feet tied together and the other end of the rope was around his neck. He had been tortured to death. They caught the two men who killed him and gave them a two or three-year sentence. I would say those men got away with murder.

Frank Antonacci was in the process of selling back his interest to his two partners. My wife was in California with our kids and on the way back, she stopped in Reno to visit Marci and Ray Sutton, the man who had worked for me five different times. Marci asked Elaine if she thought I would be interested in joining up with Ray again if he could get a new dealership. Elaine said she was sure I would because I liked both of them and trusted them.

Ray and his friend Joe Leavitt had been looking for a car

dealership in Boise, Idaho, but the factory gave it to other people. There was a rumor that a dealership in Anchorage had been losing so much money that Chrysler Corporation was getting rid of the man in charge. Nobody wanted this dealership and Chrysler was just about out of business. Chrysler offered a factory-financed deal, which meant it would not take much money down to get started.

Joe Leavitt and Ray Sutton set up a meeting with my wife and me at the Green Tree Hotel in Beaverton, Oregon, to discuss my involvement in the Anchorage Chrysler and Dodge dealership, even though Chrysler was just about out of business. Ray and Joe wanted me to go to Anchorage and see if I wanted to join them. Ray, having worked for me many times, had a good idea how I operated. He knew he could trust me, and he wanted me to be in business with him.

They flew me to Anchorage, Alaska, to check out the place, and when I saw it I said, "This is a gold mine." When Chrysler Credit gives the working capital, they only look to one principal and they will not allow you to issue any stock until the loan is paid off. Ray was the general manager, Joe was Ray's assistant, and I was the general sales manager. I was supposed to get a 15-percent ownership when the capital loan was paid off in full.

When customers would come in to look at the cars, they let us know they knew Chrysler might be out of business soon and some were skeptical about buying Chrysler products. We did have a fairly hard sell to make everything go smooth. We all worked very hard and put in many long hours. My family was in Oregon City, so I would work three months straight, everyday, and put in seventy hours a week. I worked from 7 a.m. to 9 or 10 p.m. Then I would take six or seven days off to be with my family in Oregon. All the employees knew I was joining the company as a partner because Ray Sutton told them that was how I came in.

I was a 15-percent owner in this dealership in Anchorage, Alaska.

I ran all the sales and general sales meetings as well as the manager's meetings. Every morning we would have a pep-up meeting and go over our plans for the day. Every Friday, we would have our general sales meeting that everybody was required to attend. Whoever was late would have to buy breakfast for the whole sales department and the office staff. About thirty seconds before 8 a.m., we would activate the loudspeaker and at 8 a.m.

sharp, we would lock the sales office door. If anyone came late, he would have the right to plead his case as to why. He would present an excuse to the hungry salesmen and managers, but the salesmen were the ones to make a decision, guilty or not guilty. If the salesman was guilty of being late, he would cover the tab. These breakfasts or lunches could run up to $350. The salesman could never use the excuse that they could not pay for it because we would give them a draw to pay the bill.

When I was the general manager, we had forty-three salesmen and an assistant manager. I would shake hands with every one of them at our general sales meetings. I could tell from the way they shook hands whenever a salesman had a problem of some kind. I would not say anything about it, but during his work shift, I would get a chance to talk to him and ask if something was bothering him. This was all done on a personal basis. That way, I would find out what was wrong and I would help wherever I could. I would also give him a little pep up talk and this did help clear the salesmen's minds every time. Whenever someone would call us long distance to see if he might have a chance of getting hired, I would ask, near the end of the conversation, "What are you running away from?" Some of the answers were weird and scary.

I hired one salesman who looked like a good prospect to sell cars and trucks. After Eric Schnmidt was with us for a while, I got a call from an insurance company. They wanted him to go to their office because it turned out he was one of their salesmen as well. I called Eric into my office and asked, "How much money are you making selling insurance?" He said, "Not much." I said he wasn't making much money here, either. I told him he was going to have to make a decision in order to be fair with himself and his employers. "You can work for only one employer," I said. I mentioned that he had sold me on hiring him and that working for us would give him the opportunity to make a lot of money, plus have chances for advancement when he proved himself.

His first year, he made a little over $30,000. The second year he made just under $50,000. I promoted Eric to assistant manager, which meant he would have five or six salesmen working under him and he would get a percentage of all of their sales. He really did a very good job and made a lot of money.

I made a series of lateral moves with the managers and at the time, they were not too happy about it. After a month or two of making these moves, they let me know how unhappy they were. But they ended up making more money based on what I did, and that is what I knew would come about. Sometimes managers can get into ruts. Making these lateral moves wakes them up and then they realize we did them a favor.

I made all the promotions except for the one done by Ray, who wanted his son in management. The son had been made a manager, and my other partner, Joe, had his two boys working for us, too—Joe Jr. was a salesman, and Bill worked in the shop. Both were very nice young men.

Our dealership was across the highway from Merrill Field, which was the second largest private airport in the United States. Each morning I would arrive at 7 a.m. I would have coffee with Ray in his office, listen to his personal problems, and try to keep him calm, especially after his heart attack that had occurred four years earlier.

Ray and I were very close friends and his wife and my wife were very close. His wife told my wife that Ray had a mistress in Reno. She told my wife that she would stay with Ray until he left this earth. She was not going to lose out on any of the millions that would come to her after Ray's death. The only way I knew about this was that she told my wife. I never did tell anyone.

Every month, we would set up a travel rate of how many cars and trucks we wanted to sell that month. I would talk to each salesman and have him tell me how many units he wanted to sell that month, then I would break down those numbers into ten-day periods to determine his travel rate. After each ten-day period, we would go over the salesman's performance. I always did this one-on-one with each salesperson, and the same with each manager. This way we had a clear understanding with each individual and could easily see if a problem was developing. If a problem occurred, we would help them. Without good sales people, a dealership cannot survive.

Pope John Paul visited Anchorage, Alaska.
I was very lucky to see him.

Sometimes salesmen would bring in a written offer that was too low and I would send the salesman back for more money. If I noticed the salesman was a little teed off, I would have him sit down and recoup his composure before I let him go back to his customer. Most salespeople hate to ask their customer for more money. I told them we should get the full price for our product and that they should not be ashamed to ask for more money.

While we were conducting business at the Anchorage Chrysler and Dodge Center, we found a cat that had been thrown off a pickup truck. It was starving and looked like it had been mistreated. We cleaned him up, had him checked out, and fed him back to good health. We made the cat the dealership's mascot, named him Carlot, and made him part of our staff. He took it from there.

We had a waiting room in our showroom with a television for customers to watch while waiting for their cars. Carlot often slept on top of the television. When Carlot got better acquainted with us, we would page him over the loudspeaker saying, "Carlot, you are wanted in the sales office." When he came in, he would jump on my desk and lie down. Sometimes he would not come into the office until two or three pages were made because he had been busy entertaining customers.

The customers, and all of our staff, fell in love with Carlot. He even received mail and phone calls asking about his health. We all thought Carlot was a genius. He often slept on my desk and sometimes, while I was writing a contract, he would roll around on my paperwork. One of our salesmen mentioned that maybe he did this when the contract would end up no good, and that is what usually happened. Carlot's batting average was nine out of ten, which is not bad for a cat. Carlot became a popular celebrity, which made him cocky. I worried that someone might kidnap Carlot but one of our salesmen said he did not think that would happen because Carlot would never forget how badly he had been treated before we had the pleasure of taking him in, and that he would claw the would-be kidnapper. One of our customer's children had been teasing Carlot one day, and Carlot defended himself by clawing the boy. The boy's father bawled out his son for teasing Carlot. The father did not hold it against the cat.

Ray was very worried about his son Tom, who was involved with drugs. His daughter was a drug addict. We felt very sorry for Ray and Marci. Their children had been very nice kids growing up. Many times, I heard Ray trying to get Tom to join our dealership.

Two years had passed when we heard of another dealership that needed a new owner. Ray asked me if I wanted to go in on it with him and Joe Leavitt. I liked the idea because it was in my hometown, where my family still lived. This was a Chrysler Credit Finance operation. They made me the principal dealer. As I mentioned before, with Chrysler Corporation, the principal is the only stockholder until the loan is paid off. After that, you can distribute the stock.

We had done such a good job in Anchorage that Chrysler thought we might be able to help them. I was the president and general manager, and I had to sign a promissory note for $250,000. When I was making all the arrangements to get set up, Ray said he had a real good friend who had worked for him in Reno and asked that I hire her as a favor to him. I could not turn him down because he had more money invested than I did. I was his general manager at Anchorage Chrysler Center.

We arrived at the Portland Airport and Rhonda was sitting in the lounge waiting to meet me. She was very nice and did know a lot about the car business. Ray had said she was very good at handling the finance and insurance department. The car business was slow at that time but I hired Rhonda because Ray was my partner. But I told the sales staff never to bother her because I knew how jealous Ray could be. I had to hire a used car manager to help me run the Dodge dealership. I hired Gary Harris as the used car manager. He was sort of a playboy and I told him I did not want him to get too friendly with Rhonda because she was my partner's mistress.

**Four Seasons Dodge in Portland, Oregon.
Rhonda, Dan Pistoresi, and Gary Harris at the dealership.**

My partners, Ray and Joe, were coming for a little celebration at Nendel's in Beaverton, Oregon. We were having a few drinks with some of the sales staff. A few minutes later, Rhonda comes in with Gary following her. I hoped I was wrong in what I was thinking. I noticed Ray getting irritated, but he kept his composure. Eventually, I went home to get some sleep but at 3:30 in the morning, Ray called to let me know that he and Rhonda had gotten into a heated argument and he had knocked the door down to their room at the motel. He told me he was headed back to Alaska.

The next day I had a nice talk with Gary to find out if he and Ray had a problem. He said no. He said that when he left Nendel's lounge, he had shaken hands with Ray.

Some time later, Gary asked me if we could meet for a drink after work. I told him to meet me at Trader Vic's. I was sitting in the lounge area when in came Gary Harris with Rhonda at his side. I said, "Oh, no. Please no." They said that they were in love. This news could not have come at a worse time. This was the mistress Ray had been with for six years, and he had spent many thousands of dollars of her. Ray was devastated, but there was nothing I could do to help him. I knew this would not sit well with Ray. Ray was sure I had set this up because Elaine and I liked his wife Marci. I never wanted this to happen because I knew Ray would be looking for revenge. He accused me of setting up the meeting of Gary and Rhonda, and causing his breakup with her. Not much later, Ray convinced Chrysler to cancel the franchise, which meant I could no longer be in Portland.

Ray had such a great ego, and now it was shattered to the point of defeat and this did not cool down his temper. When Ray worked for me during all those five different times, I treated him like a brother and helped him get into business. I was a mentor to him. But when it came to the love he had for Rhonda, nothing could stop him. Ray was a man who held grudges. I liked Ray very much, we really got along very well, and I hated to see this happen. I had been so happy to return to Portland and thought I would be able to settle back in. But in May of 1982, I went back to Anchorage to be the general manager. Ray, to punish me, had made me wait two months without pay before letting me come back to Anchorage. It was my punishment even though the year before, at Anchorage

Chrysler Center, we had netted over $1 million when I was at the helm. Ray never believed I was innocent of what happened between Gary and his mistress. He claimed I was the person who caused the breakup between him and Rhonda.

Rhonda and Gary did get married, but it lasted only six months before they got a divorce. I really think Gary did this to spite Ray and really did not care one way or the other for Rhonda. This whole fiasco caused Ray to have our franchise taken away.

My wife and I had some acreage in Oregon City and we decided to build a couple of houses. We were buying over an acre of land in Waverley Country Club that was zoned R20. This meant we would have five lots. Our plan was to develop this parcel of land. The prestigious Waverley Country Club course had many thousands of people waiting to join.

We did build two houses in Oregon City and moved into one of them. Our next-door neighbor told my wife and me that he was trying to get a loan to remodel his house but had been turned down because he did not have 20,000 square feet of land. He was short about 200 feet and asked if we would sell him enough so he could get his mortgage. We told him we would. He asked us how much we wanted for it. We said we wanted $10,000 or nothing. We had to repeat our statement twice more before he understood what we were saying. I said I was giving him two choices. He could give us the $10,000, or he could have it at no charge. The man could not believe it. His wife started to cry. They did get their loan and everybody was happy.

We had the neighbors in the corner, but we would never think of taking advantage of anyone in that type of a situation. This is really what life is all about. Years ago, a person I knew had a commercial building, which can be built on a property line, and the person who owned the property next door to his property hired a

221

surveyor to check out where the property lines were. The survey showed that the new building was less than a foot on the other person's property. The neighbor was going to make the man tear the building down if he did not pay him a very high price for those few inches. The man ended up paying the price to save his building. This did start many property owners to get their land surveyed.

A short time later, Ray's wife Marci called Elaine, unbeknownst to me, and said I needed her with me in Anchorage, which was not true. I did not want her in Anchorage yet. I wanted to see how everything would play out with Ray's grudge against me and his hot temper before I moved Elaine up there. I was right to be concerned. Ray knew that Elaine and I had just built a very beautiful house in Oregon City and had been living there only a few months. Nothing had ever been discussed about bringing my family to Anchorage. Ray knew of my finances because when I went into partnership with him, I'd had to show my net worth.

When Ray worked for me in Las Vegas, Marci and Elaine were very good friends. They often went to see Jerry Vale because Marci had a crush on him. Marci worked in the jewelry department at the Flamingo Hotel. Some of the entertainers would flatter her and try to make a play for her. She loved the attention because Ray never gave her any. He would lose his temper at the drop of a hat.

One night, my wife and Marci were having coffee when Ray stormed in and pulled a wig from the top of Marci's head. When they got home, he lost his temper again and broke a large door mirror and smashed out all the mirror glass. It was then that Ray decided he wanted to be out of Las Vegas, so they moved to Reno. But they always stayed in touch with us. Ray, deep down, is really a nice person. His temper is his worst enemy.

I decided that Ray had enough problems with his kids, his wife, and with himself, and I did not want to give him more problems. So, I decided I would have my family move to Alaska. We had an Open Road motor home with low mileage and in excellent condition. We picked up a truck to haul our furniture and Larry, Paul, my brother-in-law Frank, and my wife started their journey to Anchorage, Alaska. They had a very nice time and enjoyed the beautiful scenery and the drive. However, moving my family was against my better judgment. I had been living in a small apartment, which meant I had to get a house for my family.

Ronald Reagan was in Anchorage before he became president, and a $100-a-plate fundraising event was held for him. A few years before, my dear friend Carlo Apa had been telling me how great of a person Ronald Reagan was. Carlo was right. Reagan was a great man and a very great president. I am so proud to have met him. I registered as a Republican.

Ronald Reagan and his wife Nancy. He was one of our greatest presidents. I had the honor to meet and talk to him. This photo was taken by Michael Evans of the White House and sent to me.

I liked President Kennedy and no matter what party he belonged to, I would vote for him. The same was true for Ronald Reagan. That's why I voted for him. I did not vote for Senator Stevens in Alaska when he ran for re-election. I did not trust the man. After seeing the pitfalls of both parties, I registered as an Independent because they are more loyal and cannot be swayed as easily. Independents vote for the person they feel can get the job done running our great country.

I know there are great ladies and men out there that are capable of being our President. They must have the courage, knowledge, integrity, and be able to pass a strong background check. In my opinion, the White House needs to win back the respect of the citizens.

I would talk to Ray every morning at 7 a.m., giving him his therapy sessions. He would tell me all his family problems with his son Tom and his daughter Cindy, who were both still on drugs. Ray continued to encourage Tom to work for him but even the money did not sway Tom to work take the job. After two years, Tom changed his mind and decided to work for his father. Ray was very happy and I was happy for him. Tom was married by then and moved his family to Anchorage to start his new job. He started with us as a salesman, and we later groomed him for a manager's position. He was a very good salesman, but also was credited with sales he was not entitled to. I called Ray on this because it was causing some bad feelings. Tom couldn't care less.

I did all the fair practices with all of our salesmen. I would call on the loudspeaker, and the first person who came into the sales office would get the deal. Anyone already in the salesroom at that time did not qualify. Whenever a customer came in asking for me, the salesman who met my customer would end up getting the commission. Ray wanted me to give all of my prospects to his son. I told him I could not do that because it was not fair to the other salesmen. After I had a meeting with him and explained why I felt the way I did, Ray finally understood. Tom should have known better.

Ray had a problem with the McClatchy Company newspapers in Sacramento, California, which also owned the *Anchorage Daily News*. Because of his stubborn anger with McClatchy, Ray did not want to advertise in the *Daily News*. I told him to forget his anger and start advertising in the paper because we needed them more than they needed us. We did start advertising, and that helped us a lot. You cannot make a sound and logical decision in anger.

We had a lot of customers that wanted to trade in all sorts of things for their down payments. Ray wanted me to handle all these transactions. I took in a thousand dollar bill that I received $1,200 for in trade. This was a very good buy. I took in a lot of gold coins and nuggets, and ivory, and made sure Ray received everything. One day, a native Alaskan traded in more than 1,000 pounds of fish he had on his truck. We let all of our employees have their share.

I had two black Americans working for us in sales and I wanted to make one of them a manager. Ray was a real redneck and he did not want me to promote the man. I told him that this man was the most qualified of all the people we had on our force. He did go along with me and the man we promoted turned out to be one of our top managers.

We had a lot of problems with drugs at the dealership. Sometimes, when we had our general sales meetings, we would have everyone turn over their demonstrator keys and we would search the cars for drugs. When we found drugs, we gave the guilty person a chance. Everyone had been warned there would be no second chances because we would have them arrested if we found any more drugs. Tom was into cocaine, as were a few of the other sales staff. One of the finance and insurance staff had sniffed so much cocaine that it came out his nose. I told Ray we had a serious problem and we could be in serious trouble if we didn't get a handle on it. In addition, Tom had been abusing his wife and it was really getting out of hand. I told Ray not to give him too much money. Keep half out and give it to him later down the road. That way he would not have a lot of cash to buy drugs.

Ray was not in the best of health with his bad heart, plus he smoked and drank a lot. One morning during our morning therapy session, Ray told me that he would like to sell the dealership. I said I would try to find him a buyer. I said I would buy it myself, but I did not have enough money. Ray Sutton had bought the property that our buildings stood on, but he never told Joe Leavitt or me anything about it. Ray kept putting me off about giving me my 15-percent stock ownership in the company. He told me not to worry, but that made me worry more. I kept asking Ray for my stock. He would tell me that when he gave Joe his stock, I would get mine.

I was a director of the Better Business Bureau. I tried to get Ray to set a figure for the business and property. He talked to Joe Leavitt, then the three of us talked it out and came up with a figure of $11 million, which I thought was very low. I told my partners that it should be at least $13 million. I said it was worth $15 million. We had over $7 million in working capital. In 1984, we had made over $3 million in profit.

I talked to a couple of prospects who had the money and the financing to be able to buy the dealership. They wanted to buy it like a distressed sale. But this was a solid company that had netted over a million dollars every year. The prospects I had wanted to steal it if they could. I do not blame them for that. The sale went sour, and they backed off. I had another prospect who was a prominent attorney in Anchorage, Alaska. I talked to him and said that he would be wise to purchase the dealership, as it had no debt and over $2 million in cash. The attorney was very interested and wanted me to get the sale in motion.

I told Ray and Joe about the prospect willing to buy our dealership. He continued with the transaction, and agreed that after the purchase of the dealership, I would become his general manager and get a percentage of the business. I told Ray and Joe we should get at least $200,000 in earnest money to make the buyer "a liar or a buyer." This went on for a few months, but the buyer did not complete the transaction. The reason for this was he had co-mingled a trust account belonging to an Alaskan native group that amounted to $850,000. The purchase of Anchorage Chrysler Dodge Center went up in smoke. The buyer put up only $25,000. It made no sense to us to tie up an $11 million deal for such a small amount.

Ray had a friend, Art Crowder, who we had originally hired in Long Beach, California. At that time, Art was running the Chrysler dealership as the assistant to Joe Leavitt in Seattle, Washington. He was Ray's stool pigeon, letting Ray know how our partner was doing and if he was keeping sober. Ray and Art talked least three or four times each week. When we opened in Anchorage, nobody wanted to come to Alaska, especially when Chrysler was just about out of business. But when we had the Anchorage Chrysler Dodge Center going real strong, everybody wanted to join up and be part of our well-run dealership.

In 1984, I was voted one of the top managers by Lee Iacocca, CEO of the Chrysler Corporation, with over 5,000 dealers in the United States. Our dealership was ranked second most profitable, and eighth in volume for the most retail units sold.

Ray was very upset that the dealership was not sold. I was also really sorry that it had not sold because if it had been, I would get my fifteen percent of the sale price.

Six months after the sale went sour, I could feel the air getting heavy around Ray. They closed the dealership in Seattle, and Joe and Art came back to Anchorage. That was the first time Art had been in Alaska. My office was next to Ray's, and now Ray, Joe, and Art all shared Ray's office.

Rod Udd did all of the ordering of our new cars and kept track of the inventory. He was not in the best of health. One night while having a drink in a bar, a fight started and someone pulled out a gun and aimed at another person but hit Rod. He was very lucky to be alive. After that, he had a hard time with his speech. This unfortunate shooting happened before we ever opened the dealership. Ray felt sorry for him, which is why he hired Rod to take inventory and order the cars. Rod was very good at that.

I would not let up on trying to get my stock and Ray again lost his temper with me and threatened to hit me. For all the years we were friends, we had never had an argument. I have to admit I was getting worried. This all boiled down to Ray still thinking I was instrumental in his breaking up with his mistress. I was afraid he might kill me or have me killed.

One day, Art and I were playing golf, enjoying the weather, and talking about why the sale of the dealership did not go through. After we finished playing golf, he invited me to his place to have snacks and drinks with him and his charming wife. The conversation meandered to Ray and his wife. Art told me he had loaned Ray a few thousand dollars and Ray had never paid him back. One thing led to another, and I mentioned that I was having a problem getting my stock from Ray and that I was afraid for my life. I did mention something about his temper, and how he would break things in his home when angry. During the evening, Art would leave for a while, then come back. This happened a couple of times and I thought he might have a urinary problem.

A week later, after a sales meeting, Ray called me to his office. This was in 1985. Managers from every department were in there, so I thought we were having a manager's meeting. After I sat down, Ray handed me a check and said I was fired. I refused the check and said I did not need all these witnesses. If he wanted to talk to me, we could do it one-on-one. He excused everyone from the room. Ray and I were very close, but his love for his mistress Rhonda was really bothering him, plus his macho status and ego.

We had been very good friends for over twenty years. I was a mentor to him. Elaine and I had given him furniture from our house. Ray would always tell me about his problems with his kids. I was his crutch while in Anchorage, while working as his general manager.

I went to see Ray the day after he fired me. I went to his office, and on his desk were twenty guns lying there like a display of arms. His first words after saying hello, were, "If I wanted to have you killed, I have enough guns to do it with."

I was not out of line in my fear that if he did not kill me he knew he could have had someone do it for him. When it comes to greed and a mistress, and the losing of that mistress to a very good friend of mine, many bad things can happen. Ray was a very jealous person and always had to have someone stronger than he was at his side. I was his strength up to the time that we severed relations.

I never did get the pleasure of meeting Lee Iacocca, who had been president of the Ford Motor Corporation. After leaving Ford, a company he had been with for more than thirty years, Iacocca joined up with Chrysler in 1978. Chrysler was very lucky to have him as the company's president. He had a great drive and positive attitude.

I started to read the autobiography of Lee Iacocca and could not put it down. His parents reminded me of my parents who came over from Italy to be able to live in the great country of America. In many ways, our lives were parallel. Like him, I worked for Ford Motors and for Chrysler Motors. I was, and still am, in the restaurant business. I, too, was teased and called dirty names for being Italian and for being Catholic, and received a lot of dirty slurs that I would not put in writing. I am still looking for the opportunity to meet Lee Iacocca. He would have made a very good president because he knew how to pick the right type of people and knew how to delegate authority. And because he was very intelligent.

There are leaders and there are followers, and some of the followers become leaders because they get tired of following. This is the opportunity we all have when living in such a great United States of America. You do not have these opportunities in any other country, which is why most everyone wants to live here.

By the early 1980s, our dealership was making so much money that Ray gave himself a $750,000 bonus one year.

I do have to give Ray credit for how well his plan to beat me out of my 15-percent ownership worked out for him. I really could not believe what happened, especially after my family moved up to Anchorage only a year before. Ray misjudged me because he thought I would stay employed and give up my stock. He thought he had a pat hand, putting me between a rock and a hard place. I chose not to go along with his offer. My father always told me to stand up for my rights, which sometimes might be hard to do. But he said it would give me more faith and make me a stronger person. He said, "If you give in, you give in to the devil."

Ray asked me if I really thought he might have me killed, and I told him he did have a bad temper. He asked if I would come back the next day to talk about my future. I went back the next day and he asked me if I really wanted to come back to work. I told him he was the one who fired me. He said I could have my job back if I signed off that I would forfeit my interest and have no ownership in Anchorage Chrysler Center. I replied that I could not accept his offer because I could not live with myself if I did sign off. And that I would have a hard time doing my job knowing I was being cheated out of my interest that I earned from 1979 to 1985. By then, my interest of 15 percent was worth over $3 million, counting the property. I shook hands with Ray and said, "God bless you," and left for home.

I was 62 years old, out of a job, stuck in Alaska with my family, and was in jeopardy of losing all our houses and property. Alaska is a very bad place to be in when you are out of a job and running out of money. At that time, Elaine and I had two commercial lots in Lincoln City, Oregon, one acre at Waverley Country Club, three rental houses, 2.5 acres planted in Christmas trees, and the house that had been built for us. We ended up losing all of our property.

No dealer would hire me because I was suing Ray and Joe. It hit the newspaper. All I was doing was trying to get the money I had earned and was entitled to. I sold a few cars out of our house and sent resumes to places all over Canada, China, and the west coast of the United States to do consulting work for whoever would hire me for my service.

The manager at one place where I was trying to get hired as a consultant said I was too old. I told the man that I would sign a three-month contract for one cent per month salary and if I didn't better his bottom line, I would shake hands and walk away. If I did increase his profit, I would want my share of the profits.

My first consulting job was in Wasilla, Alaska, at a Chevrolet dealership, McClure Chevrolet. Wasilla is thirty miles from Anchorage. My contract was for only three months. I would have complete control and I made sure I met each employee on a one-to-one basis. The company was going down the drain. I asked the owner if he ever talked to his people one-on-one. When he said no, I told him he would have a stronger workforce if he got to know them individually.

The dealership had $40,000 out in account receivables that were ninety days or more delinquent. I noticed that some of the vendors had stopped buying their parts and were going elsewhere for their purchases. I called the repair shops and body shops that owed money to the company. I would call and introduce myself to the vendor and explain my call. I told them I wanted them to keep buying from us and said I knew that if they had the money, they would have paid us. I would ask if they could write a post-dated check that could be cashed in two weeks, and how much they could give us without hurting themselves. They might say $400. Then I would ask again if that amount would hurt them, and they would say no. I would say, "Then pay us two hundred dollars on your account now, and pay cash for new orders. When you pay off your balance, we will start up your new credit account." In a period of ninety days, I had collected over $22,000 and managed to keep all the account customers except one. Most of this success I credit to how you approach and talk to people. Always remember there are many ways to skin a cat.

I promoted a pro-amateur golf tournament in Wasilla with the pros from the Pineapple Tour. We put up a new car and a new truck for a hole in one. One of the pros was four inches away from a hole in one.

The next consulting job was in Fairbanks, Alaska, for a Nissan, Honda, Volkswagen, and Winnebago motor home dealer. This was run by a wonderful family and, again, I had a three-month contract. This operation was a very small dealership sitting on a few acres of land. Twenty-five percent of the employees were family members. The owner was telling me that one of his kids had a problem fitting into the business. He said that if I felt the son should be fired, I should just go ahead and do it. I told him that I had no intention of firing anybody, but I would evaluate everyone and make my recommendations. I said, "You can take it from there."

I took the owner's son to lunch and had a very nice talk. He said he did not know what his father expected of him and that they had trouble communicating. Sometimes we take things for granted. I am of the firm opinion that if you have a business and one of your children will someday take over your business, you should have them work at another place in a related field. That way, the child can get a better perspective and learn things that will be beneficial to your business. No one has all the answers.

Fairbanks was a Wild West town. There were a lot of nice eating-places that served excellent food. I had the chance to go to the North Pole and I got to see the Alaska pipeline that took a lot of hard work and energy to finish.

Next, I was called to check out the Chevrolet dealer in Juneau, Alaska. The owner was the brother of the Chevrolet dealer in Wasilla. They had to get permission from the tax court to hire me on a consultant basis for a ninety-day period. The tax court approved the terms for me to continue. I collected about $23,000 for the dealership. I have to say that the most fun I had collecting a receivable was when I called a mayor of a very small town. The mayor had owed the dealer $10,000 for over two years. I explained to the mayor that I had never repossessed a city before and he laughed. He said he knew the city owed the money, but no one had ever tried to collect it. He brought the cash in to the dealership four days later. I turned the over $16,000 in cash over to the owners.

But they sunk their boat, getting insurance money and taking off in the middle of the night, owing me over $5,000. All the money they skipped out with was the trust money the court had set up, but they could have paid me because the court gave them that permission. It would have been illegal for me to pay myself without going through the bankruptcy referee to clear it. Otherwise, I would have taken my money out when I had it in hand.

I even sent my resume to Rick Sund, vice president of the Dallas Mavericks, to be a PR person for the team. I did not get the job, but he did send me a very nice response.

I sent some resumes to dealers in Canada and received a call from one of them. I always quizzed potential employers to find out what problems they were having. This one dealer told me he had a manager who was not doing a good job. I asked him how long has this manager worked for him. He said over ten years. I asked, Is he honest? Is he ever late? Does he get along with everybody? The dealer said he did not have any problems like that. He said they were close friends, visited each other's houses, and their children got along well together. I asked him if he ever discussed his disenchantment with this manager. He said no.

I really did want the position, but I told the owner he should speak one-on-one with his manager to find out what his problem might be. I said that since he had never approached his manager, it was likely the manager thought he was doing a good job with no complaints. I told the owner he was not doing his job because he needed to work closer with his staff. He thanked me and said he would take my recommendation. I called the owner six months later. He could not thank me enough for the advice I had given. Some business owners forget that employees are human.

My wife worked very hard on the Exxon Valdez spill in Valdez, Alaska.

While all this was happening to me, my wife Elaine applied for a job with the State of Alaska. She was 62 years old and had never worked while raising our family. She was good at writing letters, shorthand, typing, and running an office. She was also good at training office staff. During the Exxon Valdez oil spill, she was sent up there to take care of housing for the people and to run the office. She was honored twice for doing an outstanding job.

When I got home from Juneau, I received a call from Dick Withnell who owned Teague Motors in Salem, Oregon. He had kept my resume for two years and said he wanted to see me for an interview. I went to Salem, had the interview, and got the consulting job with a ninety-day contract. The job lasted two years and three months. I could have stayed longer, but my family was still in Alaska and I wanted to be back together with them.

The Dick Withnell dealership was very efficiently run. Dave Paustin was the business manager. I really liked Salem and had not realized how beautiful the city is. Salem has some very nice golf courses, and I had the pleasure of playing on some of them. I am not a very good golfer, but I love to play.

One day, by myself, I was playing golf and I was on the third hole taking my second shot. I did not realize I was standing in water trying to hit the ball. I started to laugh and said to myself, "Either I am crazy or I love this game," and my answer was I love golf. I can do better on a short nine-hole course because I can't hit the golf ball very far, but I can hit it fairly straight.

I ended up suing Anchorage Chrysler Dodge Center for the $3 million they beat me out of. This started in October of 1985 and it took four years to make a non-disclosure settlement with them. The settlement was peanuts of what they owed me. I was supposed to get $4,500 per month for my retirement and was even beat out of that. Our loss on all the property we had owned in 1986 amounted to over $600,000. My lawyer could not work my case because he was being sued, still with the same law firm. I ended up with two different attorneys.

After returning to Anchorage, Elaine and I purchased a duplex, and later converted our double-car garage into another unit. My wife designed a very unique living space by turning it into a three-bedroom with a one-car garage. The space was divided in two floors, with one bedroom and the garage on the lower level. At the back of the garage was a stairway going up to a storage area. In the bedroom was a spiral staircase to the upper level. In this space were two small bedrooms with a bathroom between, a small living room, and a micro kitchen. Two of our sons, Larry and Paul, still lived at home with us and we found this design to be very workable.

Teague Motors "Withnell" in Salem, Oregon.

I couldn't get a job with any car dealership because everyone knew I was suing my former partners, Ray Sutton and Joe Leavitt of Anchorage Chrysler Dodge Center. I tried to put a couple of places together for a pizza and pasta setup. The owner of the property asked me what I planned to do with the space, then turned around and did it himself. It's too bad you have to tell them what you intend to use the space for. I even tried to get Burger King to take on my concept.

Over the years, I kept trying to sell my flair with Italian food to a large corporation. I had spent so much money on long distance calls but without success. I finally decided to use my head so that I could talk to someone who could make a decision. I called Pepsi Cola and told the operator I wanted to speak person-to-person with someone who could write a check for $2 million, one signature only. The operator went through several people, and I overheard one executive answer that he could sign for up to $5 million. I explained that I had a concept they could use. I told him I had presented the idea to Pizza Hut before that company had been bought out by Pepsi. I said Pizza Hut had been extremely interested in it after tasting my spaghetti sauce and lasagna. The executive told me that they had chefs from all over the country. I said I was so confident in my products that I would put money up that my food would place first or second in a taste test against any four chefs he chose. He told me they did not do business that way. I replied that since he had some idiot on the phone with a sound concept, was he not curious to at least taste what I had to offer? He said no.

I am sure he does not receive too many calls like the one I made to him. If I had been on the other end of the line, I would have explored any type of call like the one I made. I know he did not have all the answers and I do know if he would have learned a little more if he would have given me the time of day. Some CEOs are afraid to make decisions because they might rock the boat and fall out.

I called Domino's Pizza and tried to sell them on my idea and they gave me the runaround. Two weeks later, I received a letter from them stating that if they did what I was asking them to do, I would have no claim to the idea. This was a disclaimer. Two days after that, I received the same type of disclaimer from their marketing division. They might appropriate the idea but they could not steal the flavor. My spaghetti recipe was 80 percent my mother's and 20 percent created by my own sensitive palate for food. I love the food business and I have so many ideas that would help many large corporations.

While living in Anchorage, I got involved in politics. If I liked the person running for office, and was not afraid to make a commitment, I would work for that person. The governor's race was coming up and we had three good people running: Tony Knowles, a Democrat; Arlis Sturgelewski, a Republican; and Walter Hickel, an Independent. We all wanted Walter Hickel to win, but he had switched from Republican to Independent and made it a three-way race. Hickel was elected governor of Alaska and served as interior secretary under President Richard Nixon until he was dismissed for sending Nixon a letter critical of his handling of student protests after the deadly National Guard shootings at Kent State University and the U.S. invasion of Cambodia.

I worked very hard helping Mr. Hickel get elected to the governorship. My wife and I were invited to the Governor's Ball in Anchorage and the ball in Kodiak where it rains at least 250 days a year. We really had a nice time and met some very nice people. The governor's wife, Erma Lee Hickel, was extremely charming.

Walter Hickel owned the Captain Cook Hotel in Anchorage and I hung out there a lot. Bob Erneste was the manager of one of the bars and restaurant and he became a very good friend of mine. Bob introduced me to Olivia Newton John and her husband one day. She was such a charming person. Bob Erneste ran the Iditarod, and, during one run, he got stuck and hurt himself. Robert Hickel, the governor's son, stopped to help Bob and lost his opportunity to finish the race. Bob was sent to the hospital and we were very worried for him, but he ended up in good shape.

We have so many people who get elected to a government office, especially at the White House, and in most cases, they are semi-honest. Then, all of a sudden, they think they are little tin gods. I think most of our elected officials become phonies and end up with too much power. They lose their common sense and spend too much time feathering their own nests.

When I was very young and played softball at Powell Park in Portland, we had a park director by the name of Dave Epps. He was really a great person and we all respected him. He worked for Cohen Brothers Furniture Store and after a while decided to go into politics. When he ran for office, I campaigned for him even though I was only 13 years old. I passed out leaflets, and talked with everybody that gave me a chance to speak. I told them how nice and fair Dave Epps had been with all of us when he served as park director.

Today, where are these types of people who can be trusted? There are a lot of you out there, so I ask, please get involved in trying to save our beautiful country. No matter what party you belong to, just be honest with yourself and the citizens that help put you in office.

SENATOR
ARLISS STURGULEWSKI

2957 SHELDON JACKSON
ANCHORAGE, ALASKA 99508
SENATE DISTRICT F, SEAT A

Alaska State Legislature

Senate

While in Juneau
POUCH V
JUNEAU, ALASKA 99811
(907) 465-3818

April 25, 1983

Dan Pistoresi
8152 Lampliter Court
Anchorage, AK 99502

Dear Dan:

SJR 1 (Rules) dealing with the Equal Rights Amendment passed the Senate on April 21 by a substantial margin of 17 to 3. I wanted to thank you for contacting me urging positive support for this resolution. As I'm sure you know, I was co-sponsor of the original SJR 1 and have been a long-time strong supporter of passage of the Equal Rights Amendment.

The Rules version had one change from the original resolution. A whereas clause was added saying that "adoption of this resolution does not minimize the state's support and belief in traditional American family values."

Although I strongly supported the resolution as it was originally introduced, I do feel that the amendment resolved numerous concerns raised by certain of the senators and resulted in a far more positive vote on the issue. I would like to ask your continued support for the Equal Rights Amendment by contacting House members to urge their passage of this resolution during this session of the legislature. Your wires and letters do help. Every poll to which I have been made aware continues to show an overwhelming support by Alaskans for the passage of the Equal Rights Amendment. Thank you for assisting in seeing this legislation pass.

Kindest personal regards,

Senator Arliss Sturgulewski
Senate District F, Seat A

Alaska State Legislature

Representative Niilo Koponen

FAIRBANKS
Box 252
Fairbanks, Alaska 99707
479-6782

JUNEAU
Room 216
Behrends Building
Pouch V
Juneau, Alaska 99811

February 9, 1983

Mr. Dan Pistoresi
8152 Lampliter Court
Anchorage, Alaska 99502

Dear Mr. Pistoresi:

Thank you for your public opinion message expressing your support for the ERA. I too, support the ERA and campaigned for its adoption. I will continue to do so.

In addition to SJR 1, a Senate Joint Resolution requesting Congress to again propose an amendment to the United States Constitution guaranteeing equal rights to women, I cosponsored and am enclosing a copy of HJR 6 introduced by Mike Miller (Juneau). This is a resolution very similar in content to SJR 1. Your support for these resolutions and related issues is very much needed. ERA still provokes strong reactions and it is important that its many supporters continue to organize to voice their feelings if this issue is to be successfully resolved.

Again, thank you for contacting me. Please continue to keep me informed of your needs and concerns.

Sincerely,

Representative Niilo Koponen

NK/LM

**I wrote to all the Senators and Representatives to support Resolution SJR-1, for passage of ERA—the Equal Rights Amendment.
I was a very strong supporter.**

While my wife was working for the State of Alaska, her dear friend Rose started going with Ray and some of the office staff tried to break them up saying he was not good enough for her. The two women, Barb and Michelle, tried to get my wife, Elaine, to butt in, but she refused. All of this talking and scheming was done when they were supposed to be working on state pay. My wife's position was downgraded as a result. When she retired, she should have been two grades higher and received more money.

All of this happened in 1994. Today, this could not happen. Neither of the women who worked in their office knew what a real marriage would be like anyway. In the end, Ray and Rose got married and are still happily married after 15 years. You first have to know how to live your own life before you start telling others how to live theirs. My wife is still batting one hundred percent. She has saved a lot of marriages that were having problems just by talking to the couple. She could have started a great business for herself but she wouldn't want any money for helping people stay together. My wife introduced four couples and thought they should get married. All four did and they have stayed married.

There were two places where I never had any intention of living: Las Vegas, Nevada, and Anchorage, Alaska. Well, plans change and I spent many years living in each. Six to seven months of the year, Anchorage is a beautiful place to live, and Las Vegas is a great place to live twelve months a year.

Our son Paul with two friends after graduating from Alaska Junior College.

Elaine Pistoresi in Denali National Park, Alaska.

Our 50th wedding anniversary.
On our way to Denali National Park in Alaska.
The best way to go is by train and enjoy the scenery.

Enjoying Denali National Park on our 50th wedding anniversary.
A must see if you haven't been there.

Dan Pistoresi
Pioneer's Home Advisory Board Member
P.O. Box 240646
Anchorage, AK 99 524-0646
Phone: (907) 274-337
Fax: (907) 274-6940

Governor Tony Knowles
P.O. Box 110001
Juneau, AK 99811-0001

Honorable Tony Knowles:

I was appointed to the Pioneer Homes Advisory Board by your predecessor, Governor Walter Hickel. I want to thank you very much for keeping me in this position. My term expires in 1998.

This letter is to inform you that with my deepest regrets I must resign from this Board, effective date being January 15, 1996. Because I cannot give 100% effort and devotion to this most worthy division, in my heart I feel that it is not fair to you and the State of Alaska to continue on this board.

Commissioner Mark Boyer is a fine and worthy person. His Deputy Director, James L. Kohn is, without a doubt, the most devoted, knowledgeable person you could have. I had the pleasure of visiting all of the Pioneer Homes and Mr. Kohn handled the meetings in the most professional manner. Mr. Amos "Joe" Alter, the Chair person did a very good job as well as all of the other members of the board.

It has been a pleasure to be on board with all of these wonderful people.

God bless you in all your endeavors as Governor of this great State. You are doing a great job!

Sincerely,

Dan Pistoresi,

DP:m
cc:
Mark Boyer, Commissioner
James L. Kohn, Dep Dir, Div of Senior Services
John Vowell, Adm, APH
Amos "Joe" Alter, Chair

Resignation Letter from Pioneer Homes Advisory Board.

Left to right: Ruth, my mother-in-law, my mother Catherine, and
my sister Sara.

My brother-in-law Robert Albert, my wife Elaine, daughter-in-law Debbie,
and our son Michael.

Elaine and I were planning to get a restaurant on the coast of Oregon, which is the most beautiful coastline in the Pacific Northwest. My normal hangout was the Beef and Sea Restaurant and Night Club owned by my friend, George Kalas, a very generous man. For many years, George put on Thanksgiving dinners for more than 800 people. He provided these full-course dinners to anyone in need or just hungry. Whatever was left he gave to the last people served. He let a lot of us help serve the hungry. It made us feel good to have the privilege of helping George put on this feast. George had a banquet room downstairs with a pool table. We would play 9-Ball, which is a lot of fun.

One night when I was having a beer at the bar, I went to the restroom but found out I could not urinate. I panicked and worried because nothing like this had ever happened to me. I went right home to take a shower and then went to the Emergency Room at the hospital to have a catheter put in so I could urinate and that was such a relief. I was put on Hytrin and had to wear a bag for five days and then check in with a doctor I did not know. He came out and said I needed an operation. I said I did not want him to operate on me.

Then I called the Portland Clinic to make an appointment with Dr. Zoubek, a female urologist, but she no longer worked there. I asked where she had gone, but they would not tell me. I said that Dr. Zoubek was the only doctor I want to see because I had come all the way from Anchorage, Alaska to see her. They did give me her phone number.

Elaine and I looked at every restaurant for sale on the Oregon coast, all the way down to the California border. We did this twice between 1990 and 1996. We also looked in Salem, Ashland, and Albany, Oregon, plus in Maricopa and the Napa Valley in California, and other places nearby.

We had two commercial lots in Lincoln City, Oregon, across the street from the ocean. We planned to use one lot to build a restaurant and living quarters. At that time, we were still living in Anchorage and trying to get something going from there. The project was going to cost too much money, so we decided not to build.

Elaine and I left Alaska and headed to Lincoln City. We were still looking for a restaurant, but could not put anything together. I was ready to give it up for awhile. We still owned the two commercial lots. I picked up a newspaper from Newport, Oregon, and saw an ad that read, "Restaurant with living quarters available for sale or lease." There was only a box number to respond to, no other information. I wrote to the box and mentioned we were interested in seeing the place that had been advertised.

I received a call back. The owner, Maryann Binger, was calling from Roseville, California. I asked her where the restaurant was located and she gave me an address right on the ocean in Depoe Bay, just a few miles south of Lincoln City. She said not to bother the restaurant operators. The living quarters were located below the restaurant but we weren't able to see the space because the tenants would still be there for a couple more weeks. She said that the living quarters were very nice and clean.

I called her in California to find out what the lease payments would be. She said she wanted $2,600 per month for a five-year lease. I told her I would not be interested unless we would have an option to purchase the property. She said that she would have to talk to her tax consultant. She mentioned that she did not know what to ask for the property. I mentioned she could ask $25,000 over the appraised value to come up with a figure. I suggested we each come up with a figure from our own appraiser and find an uninterested party to give a third figure.

I was prepared to offer $25,000 over the highest figure. She said she could not sell for two years. I understood what she meant. I knew she was very wealthy and we would need to wait two years before we received our option, and it would be for three years of our first five-year lease. If we did not exercise our option, we would lease for another five years. We were very happy with this, but ended up spending $72,000 before we could open because the restaurant and living quarters space was so dirty. It needed a lot of work and a lot of new equipment just to be able to operate.

The refrigeration units were at least forty years old. The place was a pigpen and I could not use the rest of the equipment or furnishings. I found out that the Health Department was ready to close the place down.

We did not mind spending the money because we were going to buy the building. The living quarters were bad, with dog urine on the carpets. It was downright filthy and we would not move in until it was made clean and livable. Once it was redone, we really enjoyed our place. We could seat forty at a time. If you threw a ball 75 feet, it would land in the ocean.

We rented a second building in Lincoln City, with an option to purchase the building at a set price. We wanted another outlet because we would not need a full kitchen. The Depoe Bay restaurant would serve as the main kitchen for any location we would end up getting. We were very excited that everything was going well. We had our restaurant, which was really nice and clean, and the Health Department said we had done a terrific job in getting the restaurant looking so good.

My wife wanted a one-foot elevation in our dining area so everyone in the restaurant would have an unobstructed view of the ocean. We had a wrought iron rail installed so no customer could fall.

Mr. P's in Depoe Bay, Oregon.
We lived below the restaurant.

Backyard to our restaurant.
One of the best views on the Pacific Coast.

Elaine at the remodeling of Mr. P's, our restaurant in Depoe Bay, Oregon.

After the remodel.

We had so many setbacks before we could open our restaurant.
Problems with underground utilities, erecting a sign, and we had to build a
complete kitchen.

Left to right: My wife Elaine, our daughter Danise, our cousin Danielle
visiting from Italy, and our granddaughter Vanessa.

A NEW YORK MINUTE is all it takes to order a great meal and help survivors of the World Trade Center tragedy. Above, Dan Pistorisi dishes at Mr. P's, one of 13 restaurants participating Oct. 11 in "Dine Out Depoe Bay!" See details, Page 10.

DEPOE BAY CHEFS DISH-UP RELIEF FOR NYC TRAGEDY!

We have filled many guest books, signed by people from all over the world. We started the first guest book in 1997 in Depoe Bay, Oregon. We could seat about forty customers, and everyone had an ocean view. The food we served was the best. This is not bragging, because our customers did the bragging for us.

One of our customers wanted to have her photo taken with us. She was visiting from Connecticut.

A couple of months after we opened our Depoe Bay restaurant, I went out to get supplies. I was pushing my cart to the check stand when someone ran a cart in front of me, which caused me to fall. I put my arm over my head so I would not fall on my head. I shattered my elbow and they took me to the hospital nearby. I had wanted to go to the Providence St. Vincent's in Portland, but the doctor who checked me out, Dr. Gerald Butler, said it could be dangerous to take the chance on going that far, seeing how badly shattered my elbow was. He was not trying to talk me out of going to Portland; he was just letting me know the danger that could arise. I told him that the way he explained everything, I felt comfortable with him handling the operation.

When they did the X-rays before Dr. Butler operated on me, it was very painful. The operation took place at Samaritan Pacific Hospital in Newport, Oregon. Dr. Butler had to put a 4.5-inch bolt in my elbow. He did an outstanding job. I was 74 years old when this happened, and I am 88 years old as of this writing. I have had no problems with my elbow or arm. I started to lift weights after I was all healed.

A year after opening the restaurant, our sewer backed up and we had to close for a couple of days. We ended up with a lot of plumbing expenses that should have been the owner's responsibility, but we covered the cost. Our water bill had been a little over $2,000 the first year. Then it jumped to over $7,000 the next year. We had a major water leak.

After two years and one month, we called the owner, Maryann Binger, and asked her to come to the restaurant. She arrived with her brother. We told her we wanted to exercise our option for the last three years of our five-year lease. She said she had never agreed to those terms. Her brother, Don Robinson, said that she had mentioned the $25,000 figure to him, and she shot back telling him to "Shut up." He could not have known anything about $25,000 if she had not mentioned it to him. The figure did not come out of the sky, and he sure never made it up.

I realized I was dealing with a liar and a cheat. Then I found out she was a real estate broker in California, and a real estate broker in Oregon. She had never disclosed this information.

This news was really hard on my family and we decided to sell our restaurant because we could not, and did not want to keep doing business with someone who lied and cheated. We did not want to sell our very well established business, but it would be a nightmare to keep doing business with this woman. I put an ad in the *Oregonian* newspaper to sell our business and equipment. I had a lot of responses to the ad. One potential buyer wanted to talk to the property owner, which was none of her business since I was still responsible for the lease. The potential buyer told me he did not want to deal with our lessor and backed out.

I hired an attorney from Mt. Angel, Oregon, to sue Maryann Binger for breach of promise, then another attorney to represent us in court. In the courthouse, Maryann was dressed like a little girl coming out of the dust bowl who had lost everything. I never had the chance to get on the stand and neither did her brother. The judge was more anxious to get this trial over, knowing that my attorney came from Portland. I do not know how he ever became a judge because he was a lousy one. I later found out that many people thought that the man was not qualified to be a judge.

We made up our minds that since we could not sell the restaurant ourselves, we would let the owner list it. She had another real estate salesperson list the property. The salesperson had previously sold a house to people in the restaurant business in San Diego and ended up selling them our restaurant at half of what it was worth. We were not happy about the price she sold it for, but much happier to get out from under this liar. When the salesperson came back with the paperwork for my wife and me to sign, a curve ball was thrown to us. The leaser had three pieces of equipment we had never used, did not want, and could not take, even as a gift. A junk dealer would pay maybe $50 for these items. The leaser made us pay $5,000 for this junk. She would not let the deal go through if we did not buy it. With our desire to quit doing business with her, we had no choice. Then we gave the junk away.

This fiasco did not stop there. The people that purchased the restaurant through our landlady were starting to have second thoughts. I told them that Maryann Binger was like manure, and she told Maryann I had used the "F" word. But I had not. I do not swear and would not use such language. My wife and my children have never ever heard me swear or lose my temper. We all know how to reason things out.

The second building that we had purchased, which was located in Lincoln City, was from a Japanese American woman. Ours was a verbal agreement and she lived up to it. Her name was June Brehm. She was a very lovely lady and a person I can call a true friend.

We were starting to get our place ready to open. The location was not built to be a restaurant. We built on a kitchen, had a hood and fire suppression system installed, and purchased a dishwasher, sinks, stove, and everything else needed to operate a restaurant. Just before we were ready to open, the city tore up the sidewalk in front of our place so they could move the utilities underground. This put us back for a long period before we could open.

One night, when I was walking home, I was hit by a car that knocked me to the ground. The driver took off. I picked myself up and could see that up the street the driver had stopped, started to drive away, then came to a full stop again. I was having a hard time walking to his car because by then it was a block down the road. When I was about 25 feet away from the car, the driver jumped out like a maniac and started cussing at me, using the dirty language that you would not want to hear from anyone. He threatened to call the police, and I said, "Please do call them." I asked him why he stopped. He hollered back that I broke his mirror when his car hit me. I was getting a little frightened of this jerk. He did not even ask me if I was hurting. He jumped back in his car, very angry, and took off. I have to believe that his way of life is very confusing to him and his family, if he has one. Luckily, I was able to get the man's car license plate number while he was stopped. When I made my way home, I called the police and told them about the hit and run and everything that had happened. A few hours later, the police called back to say that the man had turned himself in and wanted to say he was very sorry for swearing at me.

Three weeks later, I called the police to find out if they had given him a ticket for being drunk, on drugs, or having a temper tantrum. The officer said they had not given the hit and run driver any ticket. I told the officer, "That it is not right." The officer said, "He is seventy years old." I said I was in my eighties. The officer said, "You are in better condition than he is." To this day, I still cannot figure out what he was saying. I have to believe that the man had some kind of pull with the police department.

I told the police that the way this was resolved, I would have a free ticket to run over someone, take off, and two hours later, when I had sobered up, I could call the police department and tell them I hit and ran, make out a report, and not get cited. "You better change this stupid way to handle a hit and run accident," I told them. I was in physical therapy for one full year because of this hit and run accident, which also put a delay in opening up our restaurant and made the cost of opening much higher.

We still had not opened the restaurant when I started to get pains so severe, I could hardly walk. I checked into the Emergency Room at the local hospital. I could not have a bowel movement and could not urinate. After they put me in my room, I called the nurse and told her that I needed my Hytrin pill. She said the doctor did not have it on his chart. I told her that my paperwork shows I take it every night. I hope no one else will be in a position where they have to go to the bathroom both ways and cannot go either way. I really thought I was going to burst. I was hurting so bad that another nurse came in and I asked her to please get me a catheter. She was hesitant, but she did put it in. This did give me relief for a little while.

Later, I called a nurse and asked if I could have a plastic cover under me because I was taking a strong laxative. I was afraid I might have an accident. She told me that there was enough protection under me. An hour later, my bowel movement went all over. This was very demeaning. I called the nurse again, and when she came in, the first words out of her mouth were, "You're not the only person in the hospital." I asked her, "When is the doctor coming to see me?" and she said he would be in at 8 p.m. I waited until 9 p.m. No doctor. 10 p.m. 11 p.m. I was still in great pain. I called at midnight and was told the doctor would not be in until 1 a.m. He never did show up. I think the staff knew the doctor was never going to come. I would not have had the added problem of being unable to urinate if they would have given me my Hytrin. I did tell them to check the records a second time. If they had called the doctor, I am sure he would have given his approval to provide me with the Hytrin.

Whenever some part of your body feels as though something is changing or different, like having a light hurt feeling, and it is something that has never occurred before, make sure to get a checkup. If you do not have a primary doctor because you think you do not need one, I advise you to get one. Most doctors are not taking on new patients. There is a shortage of doctors. This has always been a great profession.

Finally, the following morning, the head of the hospital came to see me and said I would be discharged at noon. I told the doctor I was still in great pain and could barely move. He said my insurance would not pay for another day. He asked, "If your insurance won't pay, who will?" I told him I would pay. I knew my insurance company would pay. This was terrible. I was still in pain at the hospital and the doctor saying my insurance would not pay, gave me the impression that the hospital would have thrown me out.

That night, I was trying to get a call through to the Providence Hospital in Portland, Oregon, but the switchboard would not let the call connect. I called my wife, and she and my daughter-in-law snuck me out of the Lincoln City hospital. I went to see my doctor, Nancy Loeb, in Portland, and she got me to Dr. Megan Cavanaugh, who checked my colon and found that I had cancer in my colon. Dr. Cavanaugh, at great lengths, explained what would happen next. She said I needed a colostomy operation.

Dr. Cavanaugh operated on me and I was in the hospital for a few days. Then I went home to rest for a few weeks. I went back to work and had to take pain medicine. I do not like to take any pain pills and try to get off of them as soon as possible. Never let them be your crutch. My own adrenaline is my positive attitude and being happy. This is my way of not taking drugs and keeping my head clear. I chose not to take chemo or radiation treatments. I talked to my wonderful doctor and she went along with my wishes.

A few months after opening our restaurant, a black American came in with his Caucasian wife and their children, who were well behaved. They were from Portland and we had a chance to enjoy a very nice visit. He later asked me for the bill and paid with a credit card. The bill was for less than thirty dollars, and he wrote in $500 as a tip. I went back to the table and said he made a mistake because the tip was too much money. He told me he knew what he was doing and the $500 tip was mine. We ran the credit card through and I went to the back. When I returned, he was gone. I wish that I could cross paths with him and his family again someday. I hope he will read this book and get in touch with me. I split the $500 tip with the cook. We were the only two people working at the time.

Signed gift shirt from our customers when I had colon cancer.
The photo on the shirt is of Kendell, Elaine and me.
I would not take chemo or radiation treatments.

We had another very nice older couple that came into our restaurant and they said they heard that we gave out meals to those in need. They gave us forty dollars and told us to keep up the good work. After that, they came in every other month to have breakfast or lunch and each time they gave us up to eighty dollars and would never allow us to buy their meals.

The people who bought our Depoe Bay restaurant came to tell us they were having water and sewer problems. I told them that Maryann Binger knew all about the restaurant. I said the only reason we sold the restaurant was that we did not want to do business with "a piece of manure." They ended up suing her. I was called to a pretrial arbitration session and had to pay $150 for the hearing I should never have been involved in. Before the trial, I told the judge I would not pay out anything. I said, "Do not send me any bills."

The new owners were never open for breakfast; they served only lunch and dinner. I heard that one morning there was a storm with winds so strong that it blew out a couple of windows. If we still had the restaurant, there would have been a lot of people sitting next to the windows right at that time. That restaurant had one of the most beautiful views on the whole Oregon coast and people love to sit and watch the ocean, especially during a storm. A lot of people, including our employees, could have been seriously injured. God has watched over us many times to give us the strength to keep going with our lives.

When I was in Anchorage, Alaska, I worked out at Gold's Gym. I would work out one hour every day, then go to the park. There, I would play basketball for a while, then go to the backboards with my racket and play tennis. When I was 73 years old, I made thirteen foul shots in a row, and six hook shots in a row. Anchorage had some beautiful golf courses. O'Malley was a nice course to play. My handicap was 29. I broke ninety once. Most of the time my score was around 104. I love the game! One thing I learned about golf is that you are never the best and you are never the worst. I counted every stroke and never took a Mulligan. Once, after playing with a fifteen-handicap golfer, I told him that I'd had more fun than he did. He asked how I figured that, and I said I got to hit the golf ball more times than he did. He laughed.

At 82 years old, I still exercise.

My stand-up exercises.

D4 ■ ■

Living SMART Health & Fitness

Dan Pistoresi of Lincoln city works out six to seven days a week at home, lifting weights for 20 to 25 minutes. He lies on his back for about 80 percent of his workout to avoid injury.

MY WORKOUT

Active octogenarian goal: 110

Dan Pistoresi lifts weights nearly daily on the KISS principle

By NANCY DOW
THE OREGONIAN

When you are lifting weights, do not overdo it. Start with lighter weights. When I was 82 years old, I was up to sixty repetitions with a thirty-pound weight in each hand. Lying down, I pull myself up, and stretch as far as I can. I do these reps one hundred times. But I was really dumb and ended up with a hernia. I should have been lifting no more than twenty pounds in each hand. My ego gets in the way of my common sense at times.

We opened the restaurant in 2005. Dr. Megan Cavanaugh told me not to lift anything over ten pounds. I listened for a while, but got back to lifting more than I should have. And guess what, another hernia. Kendell, who has been with us for over ten years, would bawl me out if I tried to lift something heavy.

Elaine and Dan Pistoresi on our 60th Wedding anniversary.

Our restaurant in Lincoln City could seat up to twemty-four customers, and we had customers from all over the country at this location, just as we'd had in Depoe Bay. Our two youngest sons, Larry and Paul, always lived with us (except when Paul joined the Coast Guard) and they helped us in the restaurant.

NEWS GUARD PHOTO BY BILL CHOY

DAN PISTORESI, owner of Mr. P's, makes pancakes and hash browns on a recent morning. Mr. P's, which recently opened in Lincoln City, was in Depoe Bay from 1996 until 2002.

I decided to get my prostrate operation and had Dr. Jaroslava Zoubek do it. She has been my doctor for many years and is excellent at her profession. She did a biopsy, and then later reamed my prostate so I could have a larger opening for urination. The operation was very successful. The only thing that changes after a prostate operation is when you have an orgasm, the sperm does not come out; it goes into your bag. You still get the same feeling. I used to have to urinate every hour before I had the operation, but after the operation, I just go normal.

I know that male doctors are very good and some of them are excellent doctors. But I feel comfortable with a female doctor. They seem to have more compassion. My primary care doctor is Dr. Nancy Loeb and she has been very helpful to me. She makes me feel at ease when I talk to her, and she is an excellent doctor. Do yourself a great favor and do not put off getting your health checkup. A checkup can help prevent serious problems in the future. Sometimes we put off the most important priorities of taking care of our health. Just ask me.

When I was in the hospital and could not work for over a month, our faithful employee, Kendell, stepped up and did a great job running the restaurant and cooking up a storm. This is what a loyal employee will do. There are a lot of loyal employees out there.

Our son Paul was working at Old Navy and then went to work for Grocery Outlet in Lincoln City. Paul was not one to complain about anything. He was the type of person that if someone sent him a box of horse manure for Christmas, his comment would be, "The horse must have gotten away." This was Paul all over.

My wife Elaine and I always tried to get Paul to get a checkup, but he figured that he did not need one because he was never sick and felt very healthy. One day, he said his right leg had been giving him a problem. We advised him to go see a doctor, but he said he did not want to miss work. That was how loyal Paul was to his employer. You cannot buy this type of loyalty. But his leg got worse and we made him go to the hospital. We took him to the Oregon Health Sciences University Hospital in Portland.

When we arrived there, Paul could hardly get out of the car. They put him in a wheelchair and got him admitted. After his X-rays and exams, Paul was resting on a gurney. The doctor and nurse came in to talk to Paul to tell him the results. The doctor said he had two to six months to live. After hearing this, I broke down and cried. This was the worst news I had ever heard. They put me on a gurney and checked me out and made me stay overnight. When they took me out of his room, Paul told the doctor to make sure they took good care of me. At a time like this, he worried for me, not for himself. I mentioned to them that I had to get back to Lincoln City and they said, "If you go, he goes."

They operated on Paul and he became paralyzed in his lower body. After a few days in the hospital, he was transferred to a rehab center in McMinnville, Oregon. He was there for a few weeks, but he wanted to be closer to home. They admitted him to the Samaritan Rehab Center in Lincoln City, where they took really good care of Paul. They gave him whatever he needed. I do praise them very much for the attention they gave Paul.

Our daughter Danise did so much for Paul, handling everything for him and being a loving sister. His brothers, Michael and Larry, went to see him all the time. We visited Paul every day, except for the two days we missed. Danise's unselfish devotion to her brother made a great difference in helping Paul live a little longer. Our son, Michael, and his wife Debbie helped Paul a lot.

We had a customer who came into our restaurant just about every day. His name is Roger Grider, and he is an angel on this earth. Roger took coffee to Paul every day except Tuesdays for one whole year. Then he would stop by during the day and take him candy or whatever Paul wanted. Our restaurant was closed on Tuesdays and I would bring Paul's coffee that day. Paul loved to play video games, and talk about business and world affairs.

Our dearest friend, Roger Grider. He took coffee to our son, Paul, six days a week for one year, until Paul left this earth.

Paul lived another fourteen months and passed away on November 1, 2009. He was only 45 years old when he left this earth. Paul was such a kind person and always concerned about his mother. His death took a great toll on our family. My wife has to be the best mother any child could have, and it is no small honor to be tied to the best mother on earth. The death of our son Paul took a lot out of her life. She cried every day for a long time and seemed to not really care anymore.

All of our children are very close to us, and their mother is their saint. My wonderful wife Elaine finally did accept the fact that Paul was gone, but not in her heart. She was much better when she realized he was in heaven. It took our family a long time before we could talk about Paul leaving us.

We value life to its fullest. Looking back at our life in the business world and all the car dealerships and property we lost, we are still winners because we had good health and kept a positive attitude. When we ended up in Las Vegas, it turned out to be the greatest thing that happened to us.

Our son Michael met one of the nicest young ladies that you would ever want to meet. Her name was Debbie English, and our son was very lucky to marry her. She is a very wonderful mother to their two sons. They both supported Jeff and Brad all through their schooling and sport activities. Our grandsons respect their mother and father because they were brought up the right way. Our entire family lives in Lincoln City.

You always worry about your children growing up and hope that if they marry, they will experience a long and happy marriage. It is always so relaxing to visit Michael and Debbie. She is always fixing something for us to snack on. We are so proud and happy how they treat our grandchildren.

Michael and Debbie for their wedding.

I get so sick and tired of hearing parents saying that they cannot wait until their kids reach eighteen years of age and leave home. Why have children if that is your attitude? We want our children to stay at home as long as they want to. Larry, our 48-year-old son still lives at home and we enjoy having him with us. He will leave home when he decides to. I have heard so many people say they cannot wait to retire. One of my friends said he was waiting to retire and I asked him, "Why not live your life first? Retirement will come at a later date." Most people retire too young. You will live

273

longer, and be much happier and healthier if you keep working. I have lost too many friends who retired too young. You have to stay active, walk, lift light weights, play some sports, and stay away as long as you can from over-the-counter medicine.

All our grandchildren together: Jeff, Joseph, Brad and Vanessa.
Joseph and Vanessa were visiting from Alaska. I wanted to take a photo of them together in Lincoln City, Oregon. I told them that they might not have another chance for all four of them to be together at one time.
We lost Joseph two years later.

Grandson Jeff and his wife Melissa with
great granddaughters Livia and Giannia.

Grandson Brad and his wife Erin with
great grandchildren Kensey and Kayden.

I personally think 90 percent of those drugs are a waste and that some of them do more harm than good. Never take anyone else's medication. Take only the medication prescribed for you. The way that you can cut down the over-the-counter medication is to stay happy, think positive, go to bed happy, and you will feel much better the next morning. Our head holds all of our secrets and thoughts. Let's just keep our head up and try to do the right things. Quit worrying about the little things. They will shorten your life. Just be concerned, if need be.

My wife started to lose her short-term memory at the age of 85, but her long-term memory is intact. I took her to have a checkup and the doctor's assistant asked her to spell "world" backwards. Elaine spelled it so fast the nurse could not believe it. But she might ask me something and a short time later, she will ask me the same thing. I treat it as if she asked me for the first time. I never tell her she already asked me that question. She can spell any word you might ask. She is super intelligent and has never been sick. She walks straight and speaks fluently.

Elaine and our son Larry would come to our restaurant for breakfast or lunch and visit with our steady customers and the other people she enjoyed talking to. Everyone who meets her ends up loving her because she is so lovable. I was so lucky to have her as my lifetime partner. She can recite over twenty poems and knows all the words to thirty songs or more. On Wheel of Fortune, half of the time she has the answer first.

I wanted to lease our restaurant to our cook, Kendell Helms, who is a very good cook, very clean and easy to work with. She has a passion for being a firefighter, work that she has done before. She is in her early forties and wants to fight fires. She passed her exam, and is now on call for any forest fire in the area. I asked her many times if she wanted to lease the restaurant from us and she always said no. The main reasons I wanted to lease the restaurant was because I thought I might need a major operation and it might be too hard to return to work. I had been thinking of opening a small restaurant doing Italian food and pizza, which is my love. I also wanted to work on this book in the hope that my philosophy about life will help people understand what a good life is all about. Perhaps our life and experience might be an inspiration to others.

Our son Larry, Kendell, and me in the kitchen at Mr. P's in Lincoln City.

This book has been in the works since 1984. I have had many older people tell my wife and I that we have inspired them. It makes us feel very happy to hear this.

My wife is 88 years young and I am 89 years young. We kiss and hug each other no less than ten times every day. People age themselves. Enjoy each day looking forward to the next beautiful day. Smile more often; it will keep you living longer. It is never too late to start something. Pray and thank God you got to live another day. Elaine and I do this every day we are on this Earth.

I have taken fewer than ten aspirins in my entire life. I am not against aspirins, and of the pills you might take, I would say that aspirins are your best choice. I get a kick out of people saying, "I have a headache and I need an aspirin." They really do not need anything, because 90 percent of the time, if they would just relax and wait five minutes, their headache would go away. The aspirin would take at least five minutes to start working anyway.

Try this sometime when you have a headache. Get yourself a glass of water and make a gesture of putting one hand to your mouth and pretend it was an aspirin. Then drink the glass of water. You will prove to yourself that you really did not need an aspirin. This is my own theory, but it does work. You have nothing to lose in trying this experiment.

You cannot believe how much will power we all have and when we think positive thoughts no matter how our day is going. By keeping that positive attitude, you will feel better and your chances of getting ill will lessen. You will live longer and feel better about yourself. We are here on Earth for only a short time, so why not try and make the best of it as you earn your way to heaven. We all have our little faults and this is why we should try to get along with everybody else. To earn respect, you must respect.

Elaine and I celebrated our 67th wedding anniversary on September 14, 2011. We still love each other as much now as we did when we got married. We respect and value each other's opinion. I was very lucky to meet such a wonderful woman. We are both in great health and have intimate relations. We are still happy.

I respect all women and put them on a high pedestal. The only women I have no respect for are the ones who do not take care of their children or treat them mean. Michael, our miracle son, and his darling wife Debbie have two sons, Jeff and Brad. Brad and his wife Erin have a daughter Kensey, and a son named Kayden. Danise, our miracle daughter, has a daughter named Vanessa. Her son Joseph is the boy who was run over by a bus when he was nine years old. The only sad thing about life is that too many young people die or are killed at too young of an age. Our grandson Jeff, and his wife Melissa have two beautiful baby daughters, Gianna and Livia.

Our daughter Danise with our great grandson Kayden Pistoresi.

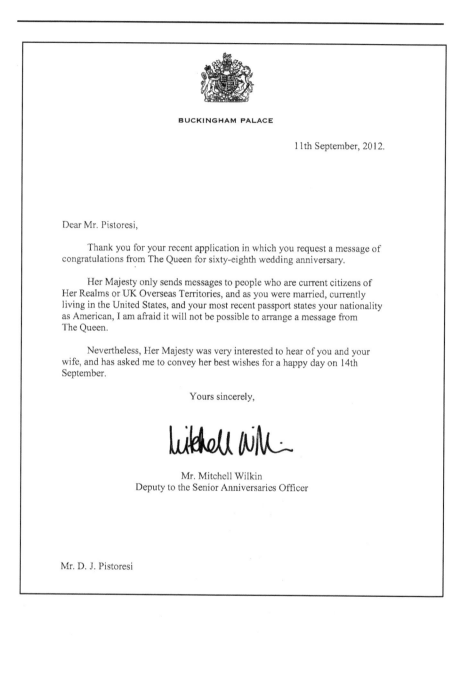

BUCKINGHAM PALACE

11th September, 2012.

Dear Mr. Pistoresi,

Thank you for your recent application in which you request a message of congratulations from The Queen for sixty-eighth wedding anniversary.

Her Majesty only sends messages to people who are current citizens of Her Realms or UK Overseas Territories, and as you were married, currently living in the United States, and your most recent passport states your nationality as American, I am afraid it will not be possible to arrange a message from The Queen.

Nevertheless, Her Majesty was very interested to hear of you and your wife, and has asked me to convey her best wishes for a happy day on 14th September.

Yours sincerely,

Mr. Mitchell Wilkin
Deputy to the Senior Anniversaries Officer

Mr. D. J. Pistoresi

Advice For Going Into Business

Where should you open a business?

LOCATION. LOCATION. LOCATION.

Location is where it is.

Check out the best and busiest corner or location. If you pencil it out and find that you can't afford the space, go on to the next best spot. Keep going until you find one you can afford.

The rule of thumb is to have no less than three month's rent (in addition to your last month's rent), plus expenses, in reserve. As an example, let's say the rent/lease payment is $1,200/mo. ($4,800), utilities are $400/mo. ($1,200), phones are $125/mo. ($375), supplies are $1,500/mo. ($4,500). This totals $10,875, which is the least amount of cash reserves I would recommend. I am speaking of a small restaurant, but this formula could be used in any business. Always lock in a three- to five-year lease, with an option for another three to five years at a set figure. Get an option to purchase said property and a locked-in price for that, too. Don't go for a Mickey Mouse-type of agreement because you will lose in the long run.

When you open up a business and start making a lot of money, and then it comes time to renew your lease, the lessor may try to squeeze you out or double your rent. If you cannot get a sound contract, do not get involved because you will end up being the loser. When you sign a lease, make sure you get an option with a set price, so that down the road you will never have to worry if the lessor will play games with you.

Years ago, a verbal agreement meant something. Today, verbal agreements will not stand up most of the time. A transaction has to be just as good for the lessee as for the lessor in order to have a sound, working contract. Always try to get an option to purchase said property at a set firm price. I leased out our restaurant and told the lessee that, for their protection, they should have an option for more time at a set figure and an option to purchase the property at a set price. Always have in mind that if you do not have all this in writing and the lessor ends up deceased, you are going to have to deal with kids and family and this is where the trouble starts.

Always look ahead. The heirs are really the worst people to deal with. One time I was unlucky in dealing with a verbal agreement, and one time a verbal agreement was lived up to. We rented a building because we wanted to expand our restaurant in Lincoln City, Oregon. The owner gave us a verbal option to purchase the property at a set price and terms. She lived up to all her verbal promises when we bought the property from her. She is really a wonderful lady and a very sharp businesswoman. If you buy any place of business that is related to food, make sure you go to the County Health Department to get a copy of the latest health report. This is public information.

My personal advice is that before you purchase a restaurant, do your homework. The first thing is get a health report, which is a must. Sometimes certain things are grandfathered in, and if they are, make sure the Health Department will let you operate under those conditions. If you get a negative response, you had better check closer, because it could end up costly to you.

Do not take anything verbal. If it cannot be put on paper, it cannot be good. Always check with your county, city, or parish because this is all public information. Cross your T's and dot your I's. Expanding too fast can cause you a lot of problems and cost a lot of money. Just ask me. I made all of these blunders. Before you make a final decision about buying a house, business, or any large expenditure, you should step back for a day or two to make up your mind about getting involved. Your judgment may be affected by your excitement and increased adrenaline. By waiting a day or two, you can think straight, and if you feel right about your endeavor, go for it and good luck to you.

We all buy so many different items and the next day wonder why we made the purchase. We have to think a little more before we purchase things we really do not need.

Gold And Silver Fever

You must watch very closely who you are dealing with when purchasing gold or silver. There are a lot of con artists out there looking for prey, and when they sweet-talk, they can get you hooked. A few years ago, I had a friend who purchased a gold bar and later found out his solid gold bar was only 65 percent real gold. The intrinsic value becomes the spot price that it should be sold for.

A few years ago, Nelson Bunker Hunt and his brother were dealing in silver and they ran the price up to more than fifty dollars an ounce. A short time later, the price of silver was worth just a little over five dollars per ounce. You can check for yourselves—this happened in the early 1980s. My personal opinion regarding investing in metals is that I favor silver over gold.

TV and newspaper ads about buying gold make investing seem quite inviting. But take into consideration that the price of gold has gone down. I am not against gold fever; I really love gold. If you buy gold certificates, make sure you get them into your own hands and do not let anyone talk you out of it. The company you deal with might go out of business, and if that is the case, you will have a hard time getting your money back if you do not have possession of the certificates. This rule goes for buying stocks or bonds as well. In today's economy, it is even more crucial to have most of your assets in hand. When you buy gold from a broker, make sure you understand the market spot value. For example, the price of gold is $1,600 per ounce. Just think for a moment. Who pays for the ads, the salesman commission, the office staff, the rent on their building, and other variable expenses? The broker's profit has not even come into the picture yet, and of course, they are entitled to make a profit. How much of the $1,600 do you really have? If gold skyrockets, you might have a chance to make some money.

If everyone purchased gold at spot, and $1 million worth of gold was sold by the brokers, and if every one of the people wanted their gold in hand within a week after they paid for it, the brokers would not be able to buy it back unless they had a large reserve of cash. When you buy gold, buy only what you can afford. If it does go down, you will not have to sell and you can weather the storm. The one thing you want to keep in mind is that when you go the grocery store and try to use your gold to pay for your groceries, you will not be able to. In most cases, if you want to sell your gold bars, they will have to be assayed and you will not be able to get the intrinsic value of your gold. Gold did go as high as $2,000 per ounce, but now it is below $1,300 per ounce. Be careful!

My wife and I purchased 200 shares of Walt Disney stock in 1956 and paid $8.75 per share. We were living in Long Beach, California, at that time. We have been trying to trace our stock for the past fifty years. Disney Corporation has even tried to help us. But so far, no good news. It is hard to trade stock when the company you bought it from went out of business. I still do not understand this because we received a letter of thanks for buying the Disney stock.

I will continue to take chances in stocks and going into business. Sometimes I come out good and sometimes not so good. No one has all the answers, but we all think we do. You have to take the bitter with the sweet.

Wounded Veterans

We all want to be protected and to feel safe from enemies that are trying to destroy our great country. We all want to live in peace and do not want to be bothered in any way. Yes, there are many radical countries that hate us and would not hesitate to do us harm, given the chance. Rest assured that the enemy never sleeps because every minute and every hour they are thinking and working out different plans about how to hurt our great United States of America.

Some of our enemies live in our country and take advantage of all the opportunities they can because they become citizens and are entitled to them. It is hard to know who they are because they are smart enough to win your friendship, fit in well in the school system, and on the outside appear to be very nice people. Some people, like my parents, came to this country to stay and become good citizens with no evil thoughts. But the enemy is working on his or her agenda of how to do us harm. When they strike, we will be caught sleeping and off guard. What should we do if this happens? I know we are well armed, but be assured that the enemy will be very well armed too, and ready.

Our service people are out there getting killed or wounded, and some are going to come out without a single scratch. As citizens, we have a great and moral obligation to take care of our wounded warriors, and for the ones who are killed in action, we should take care of their families. They are out there in battle in the worst of conditions and away from their families. Their lives are on the line 24 hours every day. We are happy they are there to protect us. But when the wounded come home, society more or less turns its back on them.

There is not enough that we can do for our returning soldiers. Some are no longer able to walk, some cannot work, and some are helpless. I was a lucky veteran who never got hurt. Our wounded veterans should not have to worry about money, a home, or how to provide for their family. They were out there to protect us. Now let us protect them and take care of them. We should take care of our wounded service people and the families that lost their spouses, instead of giving billions of dollars to countries that hate us and would strike against us at the drop of a hat. Take care of our citizens first, then everybody else second.

While I was in Anchorage, Alaska, I had an employee who was just mustered out of the service. He became one of my assistant managers at our car dealership. When I asked him how he liked the service and what type of duties he performed, he said he had been on the entertainment assignment, and really enjoyed it. He said the best part of his duty was when Bob Hope gave a show for the service people at his station. Bob Hope bunked in the same room he was in. He could not say enough good things about Bob Hope. He said he enjoyed talking to him and so did everybody else who had the pleasure of meeting him. Bob Hope was very highly respected.

My employee told me that when the government set up the budget for entertainment of our troops, they designated $50 million. He was instructed to spend it all, regardless. I told him this is not right and it is cheating our country. He said that if they do not spend all the money, the following year their budget would be cut. This is an outrage.

I am now going to talk about the military expenses. I believe in budgets and whatever legitimate budget is needed, then spend it wisely and whoever sits on the committee should make sure of what is going on.

With all of the departments involved in our military spending, they had better develop a budget. Any surplus from the military should go to the wounded veterans and to the families that lost their spouses. There should be enough to buy them all a medium-priced house, a Mercedes limo, and still have a large amount of money left over. You cannot do enough for all our wounded veterans. They are not looking for a handout and they really do not complain. Right is right and wrong is wrong.

Oh, gee. Let us send our billions of dollars to the countries that hate our guts and to people who were born in places where they never had the opportunity to think anything but hate of our country and hate of all others with different beliefs. Our country was, or is, their largest target.

I, and my family, really love everybody, but we do not think there will ever be world peace. We will always pray for it. We all have to strive to do what good we can in our short time here on Earth.

My daughter Danise with me. I received an honorable service medal from
the Veterans of Oregon (Duty, Honor, God, and Country).

Politicians

The politicians in Washington, D.C., who receive stock tips, side money for favors that they then dispense, who buy property at reduced prices and obtain low interest loans due to their position and status, often feel they have a right to these rewards. But in my book, these politicians are thieves. I request of them, please do not make this country's dire situation worse. We depend on you to be straightforward and do the job you were elected to do.

We should make all the people we send to Washington sign a bona fide statement that he or she will not commit deceitful acts while in office. This practice hurts everybody.

These statements are my own opinion and my own thoughts about how I see our beautiful country going into a sinkhole. If our own people, the ones who we voted into office and are now running our country, fail to do what is expected of them, they should get out or be voted out of the office they are desecrating.

We are being sold out by our own people. This, in my estimation, is treason. I love my country and I and my wife are worried about the future of our entire family and all of the families that follow. We all need a lot of discipline to become stronger and to be able to think with a clear head and be aware of our real enemy within. The in-fighting in our country is terrible. There are a lot of intelligent people who will undermine our country if we let them. We will weaken and then they will start to get a little control, and with their soft-sell manipulative tactics, they will influence the weak citizens and win them over without them even knowing they've been sucked in. This way is easier than having a war because no guns are being shot. They go after the weak, which are easier to persuade.

We are nice people. We help those in need. We do not think evil thoughts, but evil is around the corner. Make sure that your children grow up the American way. Make sure they go to school and study hard. As a parent, use your influence to give them the love they need and nurture them to become great American citizens by teaching them to love our great country.

One thing we all should keep in mind is that it takes a long time to build up something and it takes a short time to destroy it. I am not a preacher. I am a proud American trying to give you the facts of life in the real world. You don't need to worry, but you do need to be concerned. You should always vote in all elections, but before you vote, make sure the people you pick are the ones who will work for you. Learn all you can about the candidates. Try not to just be a follower, but if you are, make sure you follow the right person. Try to have a mind of your own and you will feel better about yourself.

Most of the protesters are paid to protest and have no idea what they are protesting about. I have talked to some protesters and asked them, "What are you protesting about?" and some really did not know other than they had been paid to show up.

Whenever you vote, make sure the person you vote for is your true choice. Be your own person and do not be swayed by anyone. This is part of your future and you need to spend time reading up on each candidate's position. I will vote for the person I think will be best able to represent me in office, no matter what party they belong to. I liked presidents John F. Kennedy and Ronald Reagan. Reagan was a true American and became one of our greatest presidents. He won the faith of the people. If you have the desire to run for president, you would be wise to take 80 percent of how Ronald Reagan ran the oval office and add 20 percent your own input. When we vote for our politicians, we are taking them at face value and some of them do not live up to our expectations. If any of them get involved in fraudulent schemes, they should get double fines or double the jail time that a layperson would get. This would stop a lot of the crooked politicians.

A pedophile, if he or she is a teacher, minister, priest, scoutmaster, politician, or any person in charge of children, should get no less than twenty years in prison and twenty years probation. Maybe, if you are lucky, you can stop one out of a million from re-offending, but 99 percent of the victims' lives will be ruined. You bleeding hearts stop bleeding for the molester. Bleed for the poor victims. Would you bleed as hard for the molester if it were your child who ended up the victim?

When you think of running for public office and you do not want any surprise attacks on your background, just bring out anything and everything that might bite you later. If you bring out all negative confessions before you start to run for office, you will have a better chance of winning than if your opponent brings it out. You will end up spending more time trying to defend yourself.

Politics is a cruel, mean, no holds barred profession. Now, Mr. Clean, make up your mind if you want to get into the arena. I believe that any city, county, state, or federal employees should have a solid background check and be able to be bonded or they should not be hired. A small town or city could be wiped out if embezzlements occur.

We need a lot of good people involved in running our great country, and I know there are a lot of you out there ready to take over when your time comes for political leadership.

I believe that for the president and members of Congress to be re-elected, they should not have to campaign for two-and-a-half years before the election comes up. A president gets elected and he has four years to try to do his job. But after the first year and six months in the Oval Office, he or she has to start campaigning for the next election. They should not be allowed to campaign until they are in their last six months in office. The President should do what he or she was elected to do, not spend time campaigning for their next term. If a president does a good job while he or she is in office, in most cases they will be re-elected.

You can stretch the rubber band only so far before it breaks, and this is how our economy has been run for many years. If our politicians were honest and cared for the welfare of our nation, and if they did the job they were elected to do, this would not happen. We know that when a politician is in office, he or she will not be able to please everyone because that will never happen. They have to do what is best for the people, not for themselves. We do have some great minds in our country and some of them should get involved to get this great country of ours back on its feet. "Dedication is what is needed."

Deflation

We all have to tighten our belts a little, and in the long run nobody will get hurt. We will all be better off. The mortgage lenders, lobbyists, politicians, banks, and unions have caused our inflation to run rampant. I like the unions; they came in to help the working class get a decent pay. This was the main reason they were needed because large companies like Dollar Steamship Line, Matson Line, Grace Line, sweat shops, dock workers, lumber yards, and I could name many more… had very bad working conditions for their employees. The owners were very greedy and could care less for their employees who had helped them attain their wealth and who had been paid very little. The unions were needed during these times, and they really did a great job.

But the great things unions did have started to diminish. The companies found out they could have their products made in other countries for a lot less money than they could when produced in our own country, even though the quality of the products were inferior. When wages go up, prices on everything goes up, and the ones hurt the most are the poor people.

One of my sons belonged to a union and is fully vested. He received a letter from his union stating that, for political reasons, they had spent a lot of the members' retirement funds. The money had been donated to various politicians running for office. They used trust money the union members were to be paid when they reached their retirement age. The letter stated that union retirement fund was 30 percent less than it had been. This money should not have been used for anything except what it was meant for.

The banks went rampant when they over-financed homes to show high profits. They paid their parasite executives outlandish bonuses. We have to stop inflation because we will be paying five dollars for a cup of coffee, three dollars for an apple, orange or a banana. When are we going to get wise and bring our jobs back home where we need them? Most of the countries that now have our jobs hate us and are jealous of us. I am a believer in helping everybody, but help us first and others last. We are the fairest minded country in the world and let us keep it that way. We must remember that charity begins at home.

I am not a smart person and I do not profess to be. However, I do have common sense and I can tell right from wrong. I will tell you that I have more common sense than 75 percent of all the people elected or appointed to the White House and our government. I am not an accountant, and it doesn't take a brain surgeon to figure out a budget. A budget should be simple, especially with the supposedly brilliant minds that we have in Congress.

When we have a problem in our beautiful country, we should work every day, no less than eight hours a day, seven days a week, and every day of the month until we solve the problem. Even though the White House has too much time off, when a serious problem arises, it should get the problem solved. We elected our representatives to do a job, but in most cases, they ignore us once they get in office. They get on their high horses and forgot about the promises they made to the citizens who put them in office. They had better stick to their words and do their job.

Social Security

The Social Security program should never be touched. It has been robbed by Peter to pay Paul. But Paul skipped out with all the money and now we cannot find him. Do you know where he is?

We have to fortify and protect this fund. It should be kept as it was meant to be. For example, let us say you receive $780 each month in Social Security payments. I believe one percent could be withheld and put back into Social Security, which in this case would amount to $7.80 per month. We all waste five to $25 every month. The next year, two percent could be withheld, and the third year, three percent and stop here. All government employees, union workers, and everybody else would receive no increase in pay for the three-year trial period. This will not hurt anybody. If we let things go the way they are now, which is bad enough, we will end up falling into a sinkhole.

This inflation is going to a zenith and we will not be able to stop it unless we do something right away. We have to level off and come down to reality. There has to be some type of a moratorium established, or we will sink our own ship. Think of the children who will end up the losers because of our stupidity.

This is all my personal opinion, and that of my wife. We think it could be helpful in bringing our beautiful country back on its feet. The common sense element should come to focus.

One more example. When our Social Security checks go up, we get $35 to $60 more. But gas prices alone erode the raise. Prices on dairy, vegetables, fruit, poultry, fish, meat, heat, entertainment, and a number of other things have soared. We are just kidding ourselves that the extra money is coming to us from heaven. Washington, D.C. wants us to be patient until they spend all our money and then laugh about it. This has become a game for them.

Inflation, inflation, and more inflation.

When you think that getting a raise on your social security check is going to help your income, just think again because really, all it does is put you further in the hole. The increase may look good on paper, but looks bad when you go out and spend the money because you will end up spending more than the increase.

Inflation is an excuse to manipulate and fool you.

This is a real amateur con game that has been fooling all of us citizens. Instead of being gutless, be your own person. We can't control all of it, but let's try and control a little at a time.

Living Your Life To The Fullest

This is how you live your life to the fullest. Learn how to get along with people and show respect to them. Be positive in your daily life and quit complaining about little things. You should smile more often because it does not take up any of your energy. And you will have fewer headaches.

Always kiss your family and give them an extra hug. This will make you closer to each other.

Before you start to say something negative, you better know what is going to come out of your mouth. Think before you speak. It is a necessity to control your temper at all times.

Try not to worry too much about stupid things, but just be concerned and aware of what happens around you.

One thing that disturbs me very much is that a lot of people do not have a strong backbone. This is something we all must learn, and we should all be aware of how our society is being swayed the wrong way when deciding what is wrong and what is right. For example, the scandal that arose at Penn State University surrounding a dirty rotten molester by the name of Jerry Sandusky. Michael McQueary saw Sandusky molest the young man and did not call the police. In my book, McQueary is an accessory to the crime. He should be fired. I hope his conscience bothers him as long as he lives because he could have stopped this dirty rotten molester.

I was a great fan of Joseph Paterno and thought he was the greatest coach of all time. But he failed at his job by not stepping up to the plate and turning Jerry Sandusky over to the police. It hurts me to say this, but Sandusky is not a human being. For all the records he accomplished, and all the games his team won, everything is eroded. He put a black cloud over right from wrong.

I would not let my kids or friend get away with anything like this. I would make sure they were arrested and I would disown them. It makes my wife and I sick that these predators get off so easy. They should be sentenced to long-term sentences, and be put where the hardcore prisoners are.

The Real Estate Fiasco

Just about everyone's dream is to own a home someday. This is such a great dream.

But the banks and big mortgage lenders went on a huge gambling spree to fleece homebuyers by loaning more on the houses than they were worth. The dumb shysters in CEO positions, and some of the people that worked under them, should take the blame for causing so many people to lose their home due to foreclosure. I would have taken care of this another way.

For example, if your payment is $1,300 per month, and down the road you cannot make that payment—which is what happened to millions of people—before you lose your house the lenders should set up a new payment so you can remain in the house.

I would have found out how much the owner could afford to pay per month, without hurting. Let's say the owner could pay $900 per month for a period of three years. Then I would set up a second loan of $400 per month for the three years. Then if possible, I would work out a pay plan to get the second loan cleared after the three years.

This will help the homebuyer because he or she would not have to move, would not have to take their children out of school, and would not have to leave their friends. They would not lose their pride. My plan would not stop all homes from being lost, but with my simple formula, at least 75 percent of the homes that were lost could have been saved.

Maybe this idea is too simple for these so-called brains. They might have brains, but I assure you they do not have common sense. The worst part about this big fiasco is that all the CEOs and top management were way overpaid for all the blunders they made. They should not have received any bonus money. I would excuse them a little if they had refused the bonuses they did not deserve, and chalk it up to their stupid way of handling their position. The public would have had more respect for them. There is a lot of better talent out there that could, and would, have done a better job than what they did, for a lot less money. When you hold down a highly responsible position that affects the country and its citizens, you have an obligation to be honest and fair on making sound judgment calls.

Wake Up Call

As a country, we are getting shortsighted on discipline.

We are becoming a weak nation that has no right to become second- or third-rated. We have to take steps to get our strength back in case of invasion. We can be ready for whatever the situation calls for.

I hope this will never happen, and maybe we need to be invaded so that we can be taught a lesson. The lesson is that we let our guard down because we allowed ourselves to become weak. We can no longer protect ourselves.

Our strength or weakness starts in the home. Brainwashing no doubt starts in the way our children are raised and how they are taught in schools. Adolph Hitler is the greatest example of how to brainwash children. He made spies out of children so that they would report their own family members and friends. In most cases, the children did not really know the harm they were doing. Some of the families were put to death because their own children acted as spies.

Brainwashing is one of the strongest tools that can be used, and it is at our doorsteps. Turn this around—brainwash your children with love and let them know how deeply you care for them. This way, in most cases, they will learn to have a mind of their own and become strong citizens. This is where strong and honest leaders come from.

Questions That Should Be Considered

Q. Why do we want to protect our country?

A. To protect our citizens and future citizens, so that our children will not live in fear.

Q. Do we need environmentalists?

A. Yes. We need them to monitor our environment—but not as dictators. Environmentalists do many good things, but sometimes they go to extremes.

Q. Why should we drill for more oil?

A. So that the oil-producing countries will have to be competitive and not gouge us like they are doing now. Oil-producing countries could put us between a rock and a hard spot in case a war broke out, and would quit selling us oil.

Q. Why do you think this might happen?

A. Because the oil-producing countries have shown hatred for the United States. They do not like us and are jealous.

Q. Why do you think we should tap into our gas deposits?

A. For the same reasons we should produce our own oil.

Q. Why is this so urgent?

A. Several reasons. Producing our own oil will help our

economy and keep our money at home. It would provides us with more security, helps keep fuel prices down, and create a lot of jobs.

Q.   Why do you think your idea is soundproof?

A.   Very simple. We have acres and acres of land that holds vast deposits of oil and gas waiting for us to do something with it. If we don't make use of these fuel sources, we could be in a lot of trouble, especially if the United States was invaded. Don't laugh—we are vulnerable.

Q.   If this was possible, when would you start?

A.   Right now because there is so much chaos in North Africa, and so many countries in that area that can't get along even with themselves, and they hate the United States with a passion. This alone is a sound reason to have everything in motion so that at the drop of a hat we could start the flow going of our gas and oil, which is essential for protecting our country. We might not need the gas and oil right away, but we'd have it when it was needed.

Q.   How about the countries we buy our oil from now?

A.   Those countries would become more competitive and fuel prices will go down. Our people will be very happy and it will help bring inflation down. This will not hurt the oil companies' profit picture.

Q.   What will the environmentalists think of this plan?

A.   A small group is really sincere but strongly against this and I don't have a problem with that. They do have some good points.

Q.   What about the rest of them?

A.   There is so much money made out of this that even those who claim to want to protect the environment couldn't care less because they make big bucks and that is all they care about. They don't care about me or you. One of their best teachers is Al Gore—our former Vice President of the USA. He doesn't practice what he preaches. And there are many more like him out there. Gore does not set a good example.

Q.   Do you think they could be bought off?

A.   A strong yes.

Q.   Why are you so adamant?

A.   Because I am over 90 year old. I have had a great chance in my lifetime to see a lot of scumbags and wishy-washy people who can be swayed one way or the other. They don't have a mind of their own. They just follow the leader without question. I am including a lot of very smart people in this category.

Q.   Why are you hostile to these people?

A.   I am not hostile. I believe in the environment but there is always a give-and-take because no solution is 100 percent correct. When it comes to a push or shove, we have to do what is right to keep our country on a sound and secure base. We need to do whatever it takes to protect our citizens.

Listen and Think For Yourself

We all have a mind of our own, but most of us never use it. We must all set up our own minds in order to be able to evaluate our own futures.

Do not let anyone else bulldoze you because you will always end up a follower if you do. If you have an idea you want to pursue, don't ask your friends what they think. I will wager that you will get more negative feedback from them, mainly because in most cases your friends will have no idea of how to put your idea into practice. Another reason not to share your idea with friends is because many great ideas have been stolen from the originators. This is why, when you get your great idea, keep it to yourself and quietly pursue it. If your idea fails, just think of some other idea. If you pursue a lot of ideas, some of them will mature.

I have asked many people how they liked their job and most of them liked where they worked. My next question was, How do you like the owner? Even the people who liked their job would say the owner was dumb. My response was, He must be dumb because he hired you.

Saved Again

On June 9, 2013, I was putting some garbage out. The porch is only four feet high, and I was on the last step before the ground when a gust of wind blew me five feet forward where I landed on a cement floor. I cracked my collarbone and cracked a few ribs with multiple small fractures. When the gust lifted me, I tried to grab onto the railing and that tore off skin from my elbow to my fingers. But it all could have been worse. Thank God I was agile, or I could have suffered additional fractures.

I was taken to Emergency at the hospital in Newport and was admitted. I remained there a few days suffering a lot of pain. Everybody was very nice to me. I was in rehab for three days and really did not want to be away from my family any longer. I told the hospital staff that I would sign a statement asserting I was leaving against medical advice. I went home and the next day checked into another hospital out of town. More x-rays were taken and I remained at that hospital for three days. Recovery has been slow but I am healing. I try to stay off the hardcore pills. I don't want them to control me.

Advice About Grocery Shopping

I want to make a disclaimer that any product I mention is something I might purchase. I am not paid by any company mentioned. I may recommend a certain product, and you should do the same if you like what you use.

Before you decide to go shopping for groceries, be sure to make up a list of what you might need, and check out the sales. This can save you a lot of money. I get very disturbed when I go to the grocery store and see, for example, tomatoes selling for two to three dollars a pound, and the next week they are selling for seventy cents to one dollar a pound. This happens with a lot of products. All products have their high and lows and this is why you have to shop wisely. You should buy one item not on your list. We all have to tighten our belts from time to time, and especially when on a limited income. Even when I was rolling in money, I watched for bargains at the grocery store.

I have some very good, inexpensive recipes to share with you. The main condiments I use are listed here. The condiments last a long time and I like to have them handy. Oregano, basil, Italian seasoning, parsley flakes, paprika, Tabasco, rosemary, salt, pepper, cayenne pepper, vegetable flakes, curry powder, dry onion flakes, cinnamon, garlic, fennel seed, onion salt, shortening, sugar, dry Chinese mustard, and instant rice. (Homai Japanese rice is my favorite rice. It is not instant, but it takes only 18 to 20 minutes to cook and it is really worth the time for its great taste.)

Other items I keep on hand are: instant potatoes, red crushed chili peppers, ten pounds of all-purpose flour, ten pounds of sugar, two pounds of dry raisins, nutmeg, cloves, vanilla, sage, bay leaves, honey, oil, wine vinegar, Cajun seasoning, BBQ sauce, tomato ketchup, tomato sauce, pancake mix, a variety of dry pastas, horseradish, olive oil, Parmesan grated cheese, chicken and beef gravy mix, and a couple of cake mixes.

Spices might be out of reach in price, but they sure come in handy when you need them. I did mention a lot about condiments and they are expensive. But they will last you a long time and they are necessary in your kitchen.

Advice About Recipes

Tuna Casserole

Ingredients: Two cans of tuna fish in water or oil, four ounces of frozen peas, four ounces shredded Cheddar cheese, twelve ounces of dry egg pasta.

Directions: Cook the pasta as directed on the package. Drain, and add the tuna, shredded cheese, and the peas. Then mix it all together. Do not overcook peas because they will lose their flavor.

Shrimp Casserole

Ingredients: The same as the tuna casserole, except use Monterey jack shredded cheese, four ounces of sour cream, and eight ounces of bay shrimp.

Directions: With these casseroles, you can sauté some diced onions, sliced mushrooms, and you can sprinkle some grated Parmesan cheese to give it extra flavor.

Grilled Tuna & Cheese Sandwich

Ingredients: One can of tuna (drained), two tablespoons sour cream, pinch of salt, four slices bread, two (or four) slices of cheese.

Directions: Mix the above ingredients with a fork. Lay one piece of cheese on the bread and spread half the tuna mix on top of the cheese. Lay the second slice of cheese on top of that, then place the other slice of bread on top. Butter each side of the bread. Heat a frying pan at low to medium heat and grill both sides of the sandwich. You can use just one slice of cheese. This is a very tasty sandwich. You can take any leftover tuna fish mixture and use it the next day. Grill it the same way.

Stir Fry

Ingredients: Take one large onion cut in eighths, two fresh scallions chopped, four ounces fresh mushrooms sliced thin, four stalks of celery cut in one inch pieces, four carrots slant -shaved thin, four stalks of bok choy cut in one-inch pieces, eight ounces broccoli cut in small pieces, twelve fresh Chinese peas cut in two, and four ounces bean sprouts. I use all colors of fresh peppers: green, red, yellow and orange. I use a little over half of each one and cut them into quarter-inch slices.

Directions: I like using a wok, but a large frying pan works, too. Get your pan ready with a little oil and throw all of your vegetables in and sauté them for a short while. Let them get a little tender and then pour in your soy sauce. Do not overcook the vegetables.

Additions: With this recipe, you can use shrimp, prawns, pork, beef, or chicken. With pork, beef, or chicken you must sauté them first before you mix them with your vegetables. With fish, you can add the fish when your vegetables are about 75-percent cooked.

Meat Loaf

Ingredients: Take two pounds of ground beef, dice one large yellow onion, one tablespoon of paprika, one can of beef consommé, 1.5 cups of cooked rice (or uncooked instant rice), two beaten eggs, four ounces ketchup, one tablespoon of black pepper, one teaspoon of salt, three to four shakes of Worcestershire sauce.

Directions: Mix this all together and put it in a loaf pan. Bake it at 325 degrees F. for one hour. You can serve this with a vegetable. The leftover meatloaf makes a very good sandwich.

Boiled Chicken

Ingredients: Boil one chicken cut up, one small onion diced, three potatoes diced, two carrots, one teaspoon salt and pepper, 10 shakes of celery salt, one green bell pepper cut in small pieces, three tablespoons of chicken base.

Directions: Boil until cooked. A very healthy dish.

Pasta

I cook two to four pounds of different pastas, and after it is drained and cool, I put it into quart-size plastic bags and freeze them. This way the pasta is ready to use any way you desire. You can use it in your soups or make a simple dish with butter and grated Parmesan.

Lasagna

Ingredients: I cook up my pasta until it is fully cooked and tender. While still in the pan, I run cold water on the pasta, and when it is cool I lay it out to dry. I will mix into my spaghetti sauce some grated Parmesan, Monterey jack, ricotta, mozzarella, and a couple ounces of sharp cheddar cheese. I stir this all together.

Directions: I use a 9 x 13-inch pan that is three or four inches deep. First, I cover the bottom of the pan with spaghetti sauce, then my layers of pasta. After each layer of pasta, I put in a layer of cheese mix. On the top layer, I spread spaghetti sauce all over, and a layer of mozzarella and Parmesan cheese. Sometimes I let it sit, covered, overnight in the refrigerator. Then I cut it into squares, heat whatever I need, and then portion out what's left and put the portions in plastic bags to freeze for future use. When I cook my lasagna, I make a lot of it because it does take time to fix. Having it in the freezer, you can take it out for a quick meal.